ARTHUR WAINFIELD

All You NeedtoKnowAboutCrypto in 2025

A Beginner-to-Expert Handbook on Blockchain, Coins, and Market Strategies

Copyright © 2024 by Arthur Wainfield

All rights reserved. No part of this publication may be reproduced, stored or transmitted in any form or by any means, electronic, mechanical, photocopying, recording, scanning, or otherwise without written permission from the publisher. It is illegal to copy this book, post it to a website, or distribute it by any other means without permission.

First edition

This book was professionally typeset on Reedsy.
Find out more at reedsy.com

Contents

1. Introduction — 1
2. Chapter 1: The Foundation – Understanding Blockchain Basics — 4
3. Chapter 2: Cryptocurrency Essentials — 17
4. Chapter 3: Decentralized Finance (DeFi) Demystified — 29
5. Chapter 4: NFTs – Beyond the Hype — 42
6. Chapter 5: Next-Generation Investment Opportunities — 61
7. Chapter 6: How to Stay Informed and Evolve with Crypto — 79
8. Conclusion: Embracing the Future of Crypto — 97

1

Introduction

Welcome to All You Need to Know About Crypto in 2025. Whether you're completely new to cryptocurrencies or have some experience, this book is here to help you understand what crypto is all about and how you can use it to your advantage.

Why This Book Matters

In 2025, cryptocurrencies are no longer just a trend—they're a key part of how people and businesses work with money and technology. Over the past few years, crypto has grown from being something only tech-savvy people talked about to something that affects industries, governments, and individuals worldwide.

This matters because crypto is shaping the future, and understanding it is now more important than ever. If you're someone looking to invest, curious about new technologies, or simply want to stay informed about what's happening in the world, this book will show you why crypto is worth your attention.

You don't need to be a tech expert to understand crypto. That's the point of this book—to make complicated ideas easy to grasp and help you feel confident in this new and exciting space.

The State of Crypto in 2025

To understand why crypto is so important today, let's take a quick look at how it has grown over the years. A decade ago, Bitcoin was seen as just an experiment, Ethereum was only starting to show how smart contracts could work, and very few people thought crypto would become as big as it is now.

Today, in 2025, crypto has gone mainstream. Big companies, governments, and even central banks are using blockchain technology to improve how they operate. Digital currencies are becoming a part of everyday life, and decentralized finance (DeFi) is changing the way people borrow, save, and invest.

At the same time, new ideas like DAOs (Decentralized Autonomous Organizations), improved privacy tools, and ways to connect different blockchains are creating even more opportunities. Blockchain is also being used in areas like healthcare and supply chains, proving it can do more than just power cryptocurrencies.

This book will guide you through these developments, showing what's happening now and what could happen next.

How to Use This Book

This book is like a guide that takes you step-by-step through the world of crypto. We start with the basics and slowly move to more advanced topics so you can build your knowledge as you go. Here's how you can get the most out of it:

1. **Start at Your Level** If you're completely new, the first chapters will help you understand the basics. If you already know a bit about crypto, these chapters will still set the stage for the more detailed topics that come later.
2. **Try Things Out** As you read, you'll find simple exercises like creating a digital wallet or exploring a crypto app. Doing these activities will help you learn by experiencing crypto firsthand.
3. **Keep Learning** The world of crypto is always changing. Joining online communities, keeping up with trusted news sources, and asking questions will help you stay up-to-date and deepen your understanding.

By the end of this book, you'll have a clear idea of what crypto is, how it works, and how to use it in your life—whether you want to invest, learn more about the technology, or just stay informed.

Let's get started and take this journey into the future of money and technology together!

2

Chapter 1: The Foundation – Understanding Blockchain Basics

What is Blockchain?

Blockchain is a powerful technology that is reshaping how we store, share, and secure information. At its core, blockchain acts as a digital record-keeping system, but it's far more advanced and versatile than traditional databases. To fully understand its importance, let's explore what blockchain is, how it came to be, and why it's revolutionizing the way we live and work.

Definition and Overview

Imagine a digital ledger, much like a shared spreadsheet, where every entry is securely recorded and accessible to all authorized participants. This is the essence of blockchain. Here's how it works in practice:

1. **Blocks of Data**: Information is stored in chunks called blocks. These blocks can hold anything from financial

transactions to medical records or supply chain details.
2. **The Chain**: Each block is linked to the one before it using cryptographic techniques. Think of it as adding a new page to a notebook where every page references the previous one.
3. **Decentralization**: Instead of being stored on a single computer or server, the blockchain is distributed across a network of computers (nodes). Each node has a copy of the entire blockchain, ensuring no single point of failure.
4. **Security and Integrity**: Once a block is added to the chain, it's almost impossible to change without altering every subsequent block on every computer in the network—a task so computationally intense that it's practically unfeasible.

How Can You Use This Knowledge?

- If you're interested in investing in blockchain projects, understanding these basics will help you evaluate their security and transparency.
- If you work in a data-heavy industry, think about how storing information on a decentralized blockchain could reduce fraud or errors in your field.
- As a consumer, recognize how blockchain ensures trust in things like food traceability, online voting, or even charitable donations.

Origins and Evolution

Blockchain was born out of a problem: how to enable secure, peer-to-peer transactions without relying on banks or other middlemen.

1. **The Birth of Blockchain**: In 2008, an unknown individual or group named Satoshi Nakamoto introduced the concept in a whitepaper titled Bitcoin: A Peer-to-Peer Electronic Cash System. This marked the creation of the first blockchain, which was specifically designed to power Bitcoin.
2. **Early Days**: Initially, blockchain was used solely for Bitcoin, a digital currency that allowed people to send and receive money without traditional banks. Its early adopters were tech enthusiasts and libertarians who valued decentralization and financial freedom.
3. **Ethereum and Smart Contracts**: In 2015, Ethereum expanded blockchain's potential by introducing smart contracts—self-executing agreements with the terms directly written into code. This turned blockchain into a platform for building decentralized applications (dApps), enabling industries to create new tools and solutions.
4. **Today's Innovations**: Blockchain is no longer limited to cryptocurrencies. It powers applications in supply chain management (tracking goods from origin to store), healthcare (securing patient records), finance (enabling DeFi platforms), and even digital art (through NFTs).

How Can You Leverage This Evolution?

- If you're a business owner, explore how blockchain could streamline your operations. For instance, you might use blockchain to trace products, automate contracts, or improve data security.
- If you're a developer or tech enthusiast, consider learning to build on platforms like Ethereum or Solana.

- If you're an investor, look into trends like decentralized finance (DeFi) or blockchain-based logistics systems.

Why Blockchain Matters

Blockchain isn't just a tool for tech enthusiasts—it's a game-changer across industries because of its unique features. Let's break down why it's so important and how you can use this understanding to your advantage.

1. Trust Without Middlemen

Blockchain removes the need to rely on intermediaries like banks or third-party services. The system itself ensures trust through its design. For example:

- In real estate, blockchain can handle property transactions, removing the need for escrow services or title companies.
- In global trade, blockchain can verify payments and shipments without banks, speeding up the process and reducing costs.

Actionable Tip: Look for opportunities in industries where trust is often an issue, such as finance, real estate, or supply chains, and think about how blockchain could replace outdated systems.

2. Unmatched Security

The decentralized nature of blockchain and its use of encryption make it highly resistant to hacking. In industries where data breaches are costly, blockchain offers a safer alternative.

- In healthcare, blockchain can secure sensitive patient records.
- In online identity management, blockchain can prevent identity theft by giving individuals control over their personal information.

Actionable Tip: If you're in a field where data security is critical, start researching blockchain solutions tailored to your industry.

3. Complete Transparency

Blockchain records are open to all participants in the network, ensuring transparency. This is especially useful for:

- Charities, where donors can see exactly how their contributions are spent.
- Food and product supply chains, where customers can verify the origin and quality of goods.

Actionable Tip: If you're a consumer, look for businesses that use blockchain to provide transparency. As a professional, think about how you can use blockchain to build trust with your customers or stakeholders.

4. Improved Efficiency

By cutting out middlemen and automating processes with smart contracts, blockchain can save time and money.

- In finance, cross-border payments via blockchain are faster and cheaper than traditional banking systems.

- In business, contracts and approvals can be automated using smart contracts, reducing delays and paperwork.

Actionable Tip: If you manage processes that involve multiple steps or parties, explore how blockchain can simplify and speed them up.

Understanding blockchain isn't just about knowing how it works—it's about recognizing the ways it can improve your life, your work, or your investments. The chapters ahead will dive deeper into blockchain's applications, helping you turn this knowledge into practical tools and strategies.

How Blockchain Works

Blockchain might seem complicated, but it's not too hard to understand when you break it down into smaller parts. This section explains what makes blockchain work, how it operates step by step, and what challenges it faces as it grows. Let's dive in.

1. The Building Blocks

Blockchain is like a secure digital record book, shared by many people. Here's how it's built:

Blocks

Blocks are like pages in a book. Each block stores:

- **Data**: This is the information being recorded, such as a list of transactions or other details (like where a product came from).
- **A Unique Code (Hash)**: Think of this as a fingerprint for the block. If the data changes, the fingerprint changes, so tampering is easy to spot.
- **The Previous Block's Code**: This links the blocks together, forming a chain.

Nodes

Nodes are computers that keep a copy of the blockchain. They work together to make sure everyone's copy of the blockchain matches, ensuring it stays accurate and secure.

Consensus Mechanisms

For the blockchain to work, everyone must agree on what's added. This agreement is called consensus. Different blockchains use different methods:

- **Proof of Work (PoW)**: Computers solve puzzles to add a block (used in Bitcoin).
- **Proof of Stake (PoS)**: People "lock up" their coins to get a chance to validate blocks (used in Ethereum 2.0).

Smart Contracts

Some blockchains, like Ethereum, can also store programs called smart contracts. These are like digital agreements that automatically follow rules. For example, a smart contract could release payment as soon as a product is delivered.

Why It Matters to You

- If you're an investor, understanding blocks and nodes can help you evaluate a blockchain's security.
- If you're a business owner, smart contracts can save you time and money by automating agreements.

2. The Process in Action

Let's see how blockchain works step by step with an example:

Step 1: Starting a Transaction

Alice wants to send Bitcoin to Bob. She opens her digital wallet, enters Bob's address and the amount, and confirms the transaction.

Step 2: Broadcasting the Transaction

The transaction is sent to the blockchain network, where nodes check that Alice has enough Bitcoin and that everything is correct.

Step 3: Adding the Transaction to a Block

Once verified, the transaction joins other transactions in a block. In systems like Bitcoin, miners compete to solve a puzzle and add the block to the blockchain. In systems like Ethereum 2.0, validators are selected to add the block.

Step 4: Updating the Blockchain

After the block is added, all nodes update their copies of the blockchain. The transaction is now complete, and Bob has received the Bitcoin.

Why It Matters to You

- If you've ever wondered why crypto transactions can take time or have fees, it's because of this process.
- If you want to use blockchain in your business, understanding these steps can help you choose the right type of blockchain for your needs.

3. Scalability Challenges

Blockchain has amazing potential, but it struggles when it comes to handling a large number of transactions quickly. This is called the scalability problem.

The Issue

Traditional systems like credit card networks handle thousands of transactions every second. Blockchains like Bitcoin and Ethereum process far fewer:

- **Bitcoin**: About 7 transactions per second (TPS).
- **Ethereum**: Around 15-20 TPS, though recent updates aim to improve this.

Why It's Hard

Blockchain's security comes from having every node in the network verify and store data. This takes time and resources, which slows things down as the network grows.

Solutions in the Works

Here are some ways developers are trying to make blockchains faster and more efficient:

1. **Layer 2 Solutions**: These are extra systems built on top of the main blockchain to process transactions more quickly. For example, the Lightning Network helps Bitcoin handle payments faster.
2. **Sharding**: This splits the blockchain into smaller pieces, so different parts can handle transactions at the same time.
3. **Switching to Proof of Stake (PoS)**: Ethereum's move to PoS is an example of changing the way blocks are validated to make the process faster and more energy-efficient.
4. **Sidechains**: These are smaller, separate blockchains that

work alongside the main blockchain, taking on specific tasks to reduce the load.

Why It Matters to You

- As a user, this means you might face slow processing times or high fees during busy periods on popular blockchains.
- As an investor or developer, knowing which blockchains are actively solving these problems can guide your decisions.

Blockchain is an exciting technology, but like any system, it has challenges to overcome. By understanding how it works and where it struggles, you can better appreciate its strengths and make informed decisions about how to use it in your life or work. In the next section, we'll look at how blockchain is already making a difference in the real world.

Blockchain in Action: Major Players and Adopting Industries

Blockchain has grown far beyond its beginnings with cryptocurrencies like Bitcoin. Today, many companies and industries are using this technology to solve real-world problems. Let's take a closer look at who's leading the way and how different sectors are putting blockchain into action.

Some of the biggest tech companies are investing heavily in blockchain. For example, IBM uses it to improve supply chains,

CHAPTER 1: THE FOUNDATION - UNDERSTANDING BLOCKCHAIN BASICS

helping businesses track goods as they move from factories to stores. Microsoft and Amazon also provide tools to help other companies build and use blockchain systems. These big names are showing how blockchain can make operations smoother and more transparent.

Cryptocurrency projects are still a major part of the blockchain world. Bitcoin remains the most well-known, but Ethereum is also important because it introduced "smart contracts," which are like automated agreements that don't need middlemen. Other players like Binance are creating platforms where developers can build blockchain applications for things like finance and gaming.

Traditional banks and payment companies are also joining the blockchain movement. JP Morgan has created its own system to make payments faster, while Visa and Mastercard are finding ways to connect blockchain technology with their payment networks. Even Ripple, which focuses on international money transfers, is using blockchain to make sending money across borders cheaper and faster.

Beyond the tech and finance worlds, many industries are adopting blockchain to solve specific challenges. For example, in supply chains, companies like Walmart use blockchain to trace food from farms to stores, which makes it easier to track down problems like food contamination. In healthcare, blockchain is being used to securely store patient records and to ensure the safety of medicine by verifying where it comes from.

The financial world is also seeing big changes thanks to blockchain. Decentralized finance, or DeFi, lets people borrow, lend, and invest without needing a bank. This is opening up new opportunities, especially for people who don't have access to traditional financial services.

Even creative industries like art, music, and gaming are using blockchain. Artists can sell their work as digital collectibles, known as NFTs, while gamers can earn and trade items that hold real-world value. It's giving creators and players more control over what they own.

Lastly, blockchain is helping with energy and sustainability. Some platforms let homeowners with solar panels sell their extra energy directly to others. It's also making it easier to track efforts to reduce carbon emissions, which is a big step in fighting climate change.

Overall, blockchain is being used in many different ways to improve how things work, making processes more transparent, secure, and efficient. By knowing who's leading the charge and how industries are using blockchain, you can start to see where this technology might fit into your life, whether you want to learn more, invest, or build something new.

3

Chapter 2: Cryptocurrency Essentials

What is Cryptocurrency?

Cryptocurrency is a new kind of money that's designed to work in today's digital world. While it can be confusing at first, understanding its basics can help you see why it's gaining so much attention. Let's take a closer look at what cryptocurrency is, how it works, and the many forms it can take.

Digital Currency Explained

Think of cryptocurrency as digital money that lives on the internet. Unlike the cash in your wallet, it doesn't exist as physical coins or paper. Instead, it exists as encrypted data on a network of computers. This system is powered by blockchain technology, which ensures that every transaction is secure, transparent, and permanent.

One of the biggest differences between cryptocurrency and traditional money is that it's decentralized. For example, traditional currencies like the U.S. dollar or the euro are managed by governments and central banks, which control how much money is printed and how the system operates. In contrast, cryptocurrency is managed by its users through a decentralized network. Instead of a central authority making decisions, the system relies on a global network of computers working together to verify transactions.

Decentralization brings several benefits. First, no single entity, such as a government or bank, can control or manipulate the currency. Second, it provides financial access to people who might not have access to banks, such as those in remote areas or countries with unstable economies.

Cryptocurrencies are also incredibly fast and borderless. If you've ever sent money internationally, you know it can take several days and involve high fees. Cryptocurrency allows you to send funds anywhere in the world, often within minutes and at a much lower cost. This makes it a powerful tool for global commerce and remittances.

Another feature of cryptocurrency is that it's often designed to be resistant to inflation. Traditional currencies can lose value over time if a government prints too much money. Many cryptocurrencies, like Bitcoin, have a fixed supply, meaning only a limited number of coins will ever exist. This scarcity is one reason people compare Bitcoin to gold and why it's often called "digital gold."

Types of Cryptocurrencies

While Bitcoin is the most well-known cryptocurrency, there are thousands of others, each with its own purpose and features. Let's explore a few of the main types to understand how diverse this space has become.

Bitcoin was the first cryptocurrency, created in 2009 by an anonymous person or group using the name Satoshi Nakamoto. Bitcoin's main purpose is to act as digital money that doesn't require banks or intermediaries. Many people also view it as an investment or a store of value, similar to how gold is used.

Ethereum, created in 2015, is the second most popular cryptocurrency and goes beyond just being a form of money. Ethereum introduced something revolutionary: smart contracts. These are self-executing programs that run when certain conditions are met. For example, a smart contract could automatically release funds for a project once a milestone is reached. Ethereum is more like a platform for building decentralized applications (dApps) rather than just a currency.

Stablecoins are another important type of cryptocurrency. Unlike Bitcoin or Ethereum, which can have volatile prices, stablecoins are tied to real-world assets like the U.S. dollar. Tether (USDT) and USD Coin (USDC) are examples of stablecoins. They provide the benefits of cryptocurrency—like fast, borderless transactions—without the price swings, making them useful for day-to-day transactions or transferring money.

Ripple (XRP) is a cryptocurrency designed to improve cross-border payments. It allows banks and financial institutions to send money internationally in seconds, with much lower fees than traditional systems. Ripple's focus is on transforming how money moves between countries, especially for large businesses and banks.

There are also cryptocurrencies designed for more specific purposes. For instance, gaming cryptocurrencies are used within games to buy items, characters, or upgrades. Tokens in this space can sometimes be traded or sold for real-world money, adding a new layer to gaming. Other cryptocurrencies are tied to environmental initiatives, helping track and reduce carbon emissions or fund renewable energy projects.

Finally, there are privacy-focused cryptocurrencies like Monero and Zcash. These are designed to offer completely private transactions, ensuring that the sender, receiver, and transaction details are not visible to anyone.

Why This Matters

Cryptocurrencies are reshaping how we think about money, ownership, and financial freedom. They provide an alternative to traditional banking systems, giving people more control over their finances. For businesses, cryptocurrencies open new ways to handle payments, especially across borders. For individuals, they offer opportunities to invest, save, or even earn through new technologies like decentralized finance (DeFi) and non-fungible tokens (NFTs).

The growing diversity of cryptocurrencies also shows how adaptable blockchain technology is. From solving global payment issues to revolutionizing industries like gaming and healthcare, cryptocurrencies are more than just digital money—they're tools for building a more connected, efficient, and fair world.

By understanding what cryptocurrencies are and how they

work, you'll be better prepared to navigate this exciting and rapidly evolving space. Whether you're considering investing, using cryptocurrency for payments, or simply learning how it fits into the modern economy, the possibilities are endless.

How to Use and Store Crypto

Once you've got a basic understanding of what cryptocurrency is, the next step is learning how to use and store it safely. This includes setting up a wallet, buying and selling your crypto, and making sure your assets are secure. Let's break these steps down simply.

Wallet Basics

A cryptocurrency wallet is a tool that allows you to store and manage your digital assets. Think of it like an online bank account, but without a bank in the middle. Wallets come in two main types: **hot wallets** and **cold wallets**.

- **Hot wallets** are connected to the internet and are easy to access. They are good for everyday use when you need quick access to your crypto. Most exchanges offer built-in hot wallets, and there are also mobile apps like MetaMask and Trust Wallet.
- **Cold wallets** are offline and much more secure. These wallets are used for long-term storage of your crypto because they are less vulnerable to hacking. Cold wallets usually come in the form of hardware devices like Ledger or Trezor. You plug them into your computer only when you need to make a transaction.

When you create a wallet, you'll be given two keys: a **public key** and a **private key**. Your public key is like your email address—it's how people can send you crypto. Your private key, on the other hand, is like a password—it proves that you own your crypto and should never be shared with anyone. Losing your private key means losing access to your crypto, so it's vital to store it securely.

Buying and Selling Crypto

Now that you have a wallet, you'll need to know how to buy and sell cryptocurrency. There are many platforms, called **cryptocurrency exchanges**, where you can do this. Some of the most popular exchanges are **Coinbase**, **Binance**, and **Kraken**.

To buy crypto, you'll typically start by linking your bank account or a payment method to the exchange. From there, you can purchase coins like Bitcoin, Ethereum, or any of the thousands of other cryptocurrencies available. Once your purchase is complete, you can leave your crypto on the exchange, or transfer it to your wallet for extra security.

Selling crypto is just as easy. When you want to sell, you can place an order on the exchange to convert your cryptocurrency into your local currency, such as U.S. dollars or euros. Once your sale is complete, the funds will appear in your exchange account, and you can withdraw them to your bank account.

Remember, the prices of cryptocurrencies can be volatile. That means the value can go up or down quickly, so it's important to keep track of market trends if you're actively buying or selling.

Managing Security

Security is one of the most important aspects of owning cryptocurrency. Since it operates outside of traditional banks, there are no protections like FDIC insurance to fall back on. This means that you need to be proactive about securing your assets.

Here are some simple steps to keep your crypto safe:

1. **Use Strong Passwords**: Whether it's your exchange account or your wallet, always use strong, unique passwords. Avoid using personal information like your name or birthdate. Consider using a **password manager** to help store and generate secure passwords.
2. **Enable Two-Factor Authentication (2FA)**: Always enable 2FA on your accounts, especially exchanges. This means that even if someone manages to steal your password, they won't be able to access your account without the second layer of protection (such as a code sent to your phone).
3. **Backup Your Keys**: When setting up your wallet, you'll receive a **recovery phrase**. This phrase is like a backup of your private key, allowing you to restore access to your wallet if something happens to your device. Write it down on paper and store it in a secure place—don't keep it online or in your email.
4. **Be Careful of Phishing**: Cryptocurrency scams are common. Never click on links in emails or text messages that ask for your private key or recovery phrase. Always double-check the website you're visiting to ensure it's legitimate. Phishing attacks can trick you into revealing sensitive information.
5. **Use Cold Storage for Long-Term Holdings**: If you plan

to hold onto your crypto for a long time and don't need immediate access to it, store it in a cold wallet. This will greatly reduce the risk of hackers stealing your funds, as cold wallets are offline and much harder to hack.

By following these basic steps, you can ensure that your crypto is safe, and you'll be ready to buy, sell, and store it securely. The key to success in the cryptocurrency world is staying informed and always being cautious with your digital assets.

Crypto Regulation and Legal Considerations

As the world of cryptocurrency grows, so does the need for regulation and clear legal frameworks. Different countries have different rules, and there are also ethical and environmental concerns surrounding crypto. In this section, we'll explore the state of global crypto regulations and the debates about the ethics and environmental impact of cryptocurrencies.

Global Crypto Regulations

Cryptocurrency operates in a global, decentralized system, meaning no single government controls it. This presents a challenge for regulators who are trying to figure out how to manage its use while protecting consumers and maintaining financial stability.

Different countries have taken varying approaches to regulating cryptocurrency. Some countries have fully embraced it, while others have placed restrictions or outright bans.

- **The United States** has a complex regulatory environment. The Securities and Exchange Commission (SEC) treats some cryptocurrencies like stocks, while others fall under the Commodity Futures Trading Commission (CFTC). The U.S. has also introduced proposals for better tax reporting and anti-money laundering measures for crypto transactions. However, the exact regulatory framework continues to evolve, leaving some uncertainty for investors and businesses.
- **European Union** is moving toward more unified regulation. The European Central Bank (ECB) has recognized the importance of crypto and is working on creating clearer rules for digital currencies. In 2023, the EU introduced the **Markets in Crypto-Assets (MiCA) regulation**, which aims to standardize crypto rules across member states. The regulation focuses on investor protection, stablecoins, and anti-money laundering.
- **China** has taken a strict stance by banning cryptocurrency exchanges and initial coin offerings (ICOs). However, it has also been working on developing its own central bank digital currency (CBDC), called the **digital yuan**. This shows that even though China doesn't allow decentralized cryptocurrencies, it recognizes the importance of digital currencies in the global economy.
- **El Salvador** has taken a bold step by making **Bitcoin legal tender**, allowing it to be used alongside the U.S. dollar for

transactions. This is a unique case, and while it has garnered global attention, it also raised questions about the risks and volatility associated with using cryptocurrencies for day-to-day transactions.

As cryptocurrency continues to grow, expect more countries to either adopt clearer regulations or make changes to their existing laws. It's important for anyone involved in cryptocurrency—whether buying, selling, or developing—to stay up-to-date with the regulations in their region.

Ethical and Environmental Debates

Cryptocurrency has sparked significant debates about its ethical implications and environmental impact. While many people see it as an exciting financial innovation, there are growing concerns about how it affects society and the planet.

One major concern is the environmental impact of cryptocurrencies like **Bitcoin**. Bitcoin mining, which is the process of verifying transactions and securing the network, requires a significant amount of energy. Miners use specialized computers to solve complex mathematical problems, and the more miners there are, the more computing power is required. This can lead to a high energy consumption, particularly when the energy comes from non-renewable sources like coal. Some studies suggest that Bitcoin mining could consume as much energy as entire countries, such as Argentina or the Netherlands.

The environmental debate isn't limited to Bitcoin. **Proof of Work (PoW)**, the consensus mechanism that powers Bitcoin and many other cryptocurrencies, is often criticized for being energy-intensive. However, some newer cryptocurrencies are using more eco-friendly methods, like **Proof of Stake (PoS)**, which consumes much less energy. Ethereum, for example, has transitioned to PoS, significantly reducing its environmental footprint.

Beyond environmental concerns, there are also ethical debates around cryptocurrencies. One major issue is the use of crypto for illicit activities. Because cryptocurrencies allow for anonymous transactions, they have been used in illegal transactions, such as money laundering and the purchase of illegal goods. While the vast majority of cryptocurrency transactions are legitimate, these illicit activities have led to calls for stricter regulations and better tracking systems.

Another ethical concern is the volatility of cryptocurrencies. While some see it as an opportunity for high returns, others argue that the speculative nature of crypto can lead to financial instability for those who are not well-informed. Cryptocurrencies can experience extreme price swings, which can cause significant losses for investors, especially those who are new to the market.

Lastly, there is a concern about the accessibility and inclusivity of cryptocurrency. While cryptocurrencies can offer financial freedom and opportunities, they can also exclude people without access to the internet or technical knowledge. Some argue that cryptocurrencies are mostly benefiting wealthier, more tech-savvy individuals, leaving others behind.

Understanding the global regulatory landscape and the ethical and environmental implications of cryptocurrency is crucial for anyone looking to get involved in this space. While crypto holds enormous potential for transforming the financial world, it's important to consider the broader consequences and to ensure that its growth is responsible and sustainable. As the market matures, regulations will likely continue to evolve, and the ethical and environmental debates will play a significant role in shaping the future of cryptocurrency.

4

Chapter 3: Decentralized Finance (DeFi) Demystified

What is DeFi?

DeFi, short for "Decentralized Finance," is one of the most exciting and transformative areas of the cryptocurrency world. It aims to recreate traditional financial systems—like banks, loans, and insurance—using blockchain technology, without relying on central authorities like banks or governments. In this section, we'll break down what DeFi is and the core features that make it so revolutionary.

Defining DeFi

At its core, **DeFi** is about making financial services available to anyone, anywhere, without needing a middleman like a bank or financial institution. Instead of trusting traditional systems that are controlled by centralized entities, DeFi leverages blockchain technology to provide financial services in a peer-to-peer manner.

The promise of DeFi is simple: to create an open, permissionless, and decentralized financial ecosystem that anyone with an internet connection can access. Whether you're borrowing money, earning interest, trading assets, or buying insurance, DeFi makes these services available in a more transparent, secure, and efficient way.

DeFi is built on smart contracts, which are self-executing contracts with the terms directly written into code. These contracts automatically enforce the agreement once conditions are met, reducing the need for human intermediaries and the risk of errors or fraud. This opens up a world of possibilities, such as creating decentralized exchanges, lending platforms, and even insurance protocols, all operating autonomously on the blockchain.

The most widely used blockchain for DeFi is **Ethereum**, which supports a large ecosystem of DeFi applications. However, other blockchains, like **Binance Smart Chain** and **Solana**, are also growing in popularity for DeFi projects.

Core Features

DeFi is unique because it offers financial services that are not only more inclusive but also more efficient. Here are some of the core features of DeFi that make it so powerful:

1. **Decentralization**: DeFi eliminates intermediaries like banks and brokers. Instead of relying on a central authority, the financial system operates through a decentralized network of computers. This helps reduce costs and make transactions more efficient. It also ensures that control is

CHAPTER 3: DECENTRALIZED FINANCE (DEFI) DEMYSTIFIED

distributed across the network, meaning no single party can manipulate the system.

2. **Smart Contracts**: One of the key innovations behind DeFi is the use of **smart contracts**. These are digital contracts that automatically execute when certain conditions are met. For example, a smart contract can be used to facilitate a loan, ensuring that the funds are only released when the borrower meets certain conditions, like providing collateral. Smart contracts make transactions faster, cheaper, and more transparent by cutting out the need for intermediaries.

3. **Tokenization**: DeFi allows traditional assets to be "tokenized" and represented as digital tokens on the blockchain. This means that anything from real estate to stocks can be represented as tokens, making them easier to trade, sell, or transfer. For example, you can own a fraction of a real estate property by purchasing a token that represents your share of ownership, making investing more accessible to everyone.

4. **Liquidity Pools**: In traditional finance, markets are often liquid when there's enough supply and demand. DeFi creates liquidity through **liquidity pools**, which are pools of tokens locked into a smart contract. These pools enable decentralized exchanges (DEXs) to provide instant trades between users. In return for contributing tokens to these pools, liquidity providers earn fees from the trades, creating a way for users to earn passive income.

5. **Yield Farming and Staking**: DeFi has introduced innovative ways for users to earn income, such as **yield farming** and **staking**. Yield farming involves providing liquidity to DeFi protocols in exchange for rewards, usually paid

in tokens. Staking, on the other hand, involves locking up your cryptocurrency in a smart contract to help secure a network and receive rewards in return. These features offer users the chance to earn higher returns compared to traditional savings accounts or investments.

6. **Decentralized Exchanges (DEXs)**: Traditional exchanges like the New York Stock Exchange or centralized cryptocurrency exchanges (e.g., Coinbase) act as intermediaries, matching buyers and sellers. DeFi eliminates the need for intermediaries with **decentralized exchanges** (DEXs) such as Uniswap and Sushiswap. These platforms allow users to trade directly with each other, reducing fees and increasing privacy. DEXs rely on liquidity pools and smart contracts to ensure smooth, automated trades.

7. **Borrowing and Lending**: DeFi platforms allow users to borrow and lend money directly to one another without the need for banks. Lenders earn interest on the crypto they lend, and borrowers can access funds quickly without the lengthy approval processes that traditional banks require. Popular lending platforms include **Aave** and **Compound**, where users can deposit their crypto and earn interest, or take out a loan by providing collateral.

DeFi has the potential to revolutionize the financial system by providing decentralized alternatives to traditional financial products and services. It's about creating an open and permissionless system that allows anyone to access financial services—whether for borrowing, lending, trading, or investing—without relying on intermediaries. With its core features like smart contracts, liquidity pools, and decentralized exchanges, DeFi is making the financial world more transparent, accessible, and efficient. As it continues to grow, it will likely reshape how we think about and interact with money.

DeFi Applications

DeFi, or Decentralized Finance, offers a wide range of applications that are transforming how we access and use financial services. These applications, built on blockchain and powered by smart contracts, allow users to lend, borrow, trade, and earn rewards—all without relying on traditional banks or financial institutions. In this section, we'll dive into three key DeFi applications: Lending and Borrowing, Decentralized Exchanges (DEXs), and Staking and Yield Farming.

Lending and Borrowing

Lending and borrowing are two of the most fundamental financial activities, and DeFi platforms are reshaping how they work. Traditional lending usually involves a bank acting as a middleman, charging fees, and setting interest rates. With DeFi, anyone can lend or borrow directly from others, with smart contracts governing the entire process.

Here's how it works:

- **Lending**: Users can lend their cryptocurrency to others by depositing it into a decentralized lending platform, such as **Aave**, **Compound**, or **MakerDAO**. In return, they earn interest on the assets they lend. The interest rate is often determined algorithmically based on market demand and supply for specific assets.

- **Borrowing**: Borrowers can access loans by collateralizing their cryptocurrency. For example, if you want to borrow a certain amount of stablecoins, you may need to provide a higher value of another cryptocurrency as collateral. This collateral ensures that lenders are protected if the borrower fails to repay. Borrowing is usually quick and does not require a credit check, making it accessible to anyone with crypto assets.

One of the key benefits of DeFi lending and borrowing is the transparency and speed of transactions. Everything is governed by smart contracts, so there's no need for an intermediary to manage the process. The terms are set automatically based on the protocols of the platform, and loans can be accessed instantly.

Decentralized Exchanges (DEXs)

Traditional exchanges like Coinbase, Kraken, and Binance are centralized, meaning they act as intermediaries that manage trades between buyers and sellers. In contrast, **Decentralized Exchanges (DEXs)** like **Uniswap**, **Sushiswap**, and **Curve Finance** allow users to trade cryptocurrencies directly with one another, without any central authority overseeing the process.

How do DEXs work?

- **Liquidity Pools**: Instead of relying on buyers and sellers to match orders, DEXs use liquidity pools. These pools are collections of tokens provided by users who want to earn

rewards for supplying liquidity. When you want to trade a token, the DEX automatically matches your trade with the tokens in the liquidity pool, ensuring there's always enough liquidity for transactions.
- **Smart Contracts**: Every trade on a DEX is executed by a smart contract, ensuring that trades are fast and transparent. These contracts automatically carry out the transaction once certain conditions are met, making the process efficient and eliminating the need for a centralized exchange to oversee it.
- **Privacy and Control**: One of the main attractions of DEXs is that users maintain control of their own funds. When using a centralized exchange, you typically need to deposit your crypto into the exchange's wallet. On a DEX, you retain full control over your assets, only connecting your wallet to the exchange when you want to make a trade.

DEXs offer several advantages, such as lower fees, more privacy, and the ability to trade any token listed on the platform. However, they can also have higher slippage (the difference between the expected price and the actual price of a trade), especially with smaller or less liquid tokens.

Staking and Yield Farming

Staking and yield farming are ways to earn rewards and generate passive income by participating in the DeFi ecosystem. While both methods allow you to earn returns on your cryptocurrency holdings, they work in different ways.

- **Staking**: Staking involves locking up your cryptocurrency in a network to help secure the blockchain and participate in its operations. In return for your participation, you earn rewards, usually in the form of the native token of the blockchain. For example, on Ethereum 2.0 (which uses Proof of Stake), users can stake their ETH to help validate transactions and secure the network. In return, they receive ETH as rewards.

The key benefit of staking is that it's relatively simple and provides a way to earn passive income while also helping to secure the network. However, there's usually a lock-up period, meaning you won't be able to access your funds until the staking period ends.

- **Yield Farming**: Yield farming, also known as liquidity mining, involves providing liquidity to decentralized platforms in exchange for rewards. This typically involves adding your crypto to liquidity pools on DEXs or lending platforms. Yield farmers earn rewards in the form of interest or tokens, which can often be reinvested to generate compound returns.

Yield farming can offer higher returns than staking, but it also comes with more risks. The rewards can fluctuate depending on market conditions, and there's the risk of losing part of your initial investment due to impermanent loss, which occurs when the value of the assets you provide to a liquidity pool changes significantly.

While staking is a more straightforward way to earn rewards by participating in a blockchain's consensus mechanism, yield farming requires more active management and a deeper understanding of the protocols involved.

DeFi applications are transforming the way we think about financial services by making them more accessible, efficient, and decentralized. Lending and borrowing platforms are offering users new ways to earn interest and access capital, while decentralized exchanges are giving people more control over their trades. Staking and yield farming are allowing crypto holders to earn passive income by supporting the network or providing liquidity.

As the DeFi space continues to grow, more innovative applications are likely to emerge, expanding the possibilities for users to earn, trade, and invest in cryptocurrency. By understanding these core applications, you can start taking advantage of the benefits DeFi has to offer and become an active participant in the decentralized financial ecosystem.

Risks and Challenges in DeFi

While Decentralized Finance (DeFi) offers many exciting opportunities for financial innovation and inclusion, it's important to be aware of the risks and challenges involved. The DeFi space is still evolving, and while it has great potential, there are several risks that can impact users and investors. In this section, we'll look at two major challenges in DeFi: **security issues** and **regulatory challenges**.

Security Issues

Security is one of the most significant risks in the DeFi ecosystem. Because DeFi relies on smart contracts, which are self-executing and operate without intermediaries, any vulnerabilities in the underlying code can lead to substantial losses for users. While blockchain itself is generally considered secure, the smart contracts and decentralized platforms built on top of it are not immune to attacks and bugs.

- **Smart Contract Vulnerabilities**: A major security issue arises from flaws in the coding of smart contracts. These contracts are responsible for automating transactions and ensuring that the rules of the platform are followed. However, if there's an error or a vulnerability in the code, it can be exploited by hackers. This has happened several times in the past, leading to losses for users. For example, in 2020, the DeFi project **bZx** was hacked twice, with attackers exploiting weaknesses in its smart contracts to steal funds.
- **Rug Pulls**: A "rug pull" is a type of scam in which the creators of a DeFi project suddenly withdraw all the funds from a liquidity pool, leaving investors with worthless tokens. These scams typically happen in the early stages of a project when there's little regulation or oversight. While this risk is not unique to DeFi, the lack of central authority and the pseudonymous nature of blockchain transactions can make it harder to track and prevent.
- **Flash Loan Attacks**: Flash loans are uncollateralized loans that allow users to borrow large amounts of crypto for a very short period of time. While they offer useful liquidity, they can also be exploited by malicious actors. In a flash

loan attack, hackers can borrow large sums of money to manipulate the prices of assets on decentralized exchanges (DEXs), taking advantage of price discrepancies to make a profit at the expense of other users. In 2020, a high-profile flash loan attack targeted the DeFi platform **Yearn Finance**, resulting in the loss of millions of dollars.

- **Lack of Audits**: Many DeFi projects are still in their early stages and may not have undergone thorough security audits. While larger, more established projects tend to undergo regular audits by third-party firms, smaller projects might not have the resources to ensure the security of their platforms. This increases the likelihood of vulnerabilities being overlooked or exploited.

Given these security risks, it's crucial for anyone involved in DeFi to carefully research projects before investing. Look for platforms with a solid track record, third-party audits, and transparent governance. Additionally, using hardware wallets for storing assets and only interacting with trusted platforms can help minimize exposure to attacks.

Regulatory Challenges

DeFi is still operating in a largely unregulated environment, which presents several challenges for both users and regulators. The decentralized nature of DeFi platforms means that they operate without a central authority overseeing transactions. This makes it harder for governments and financial institutions to apply traditional regulations, such as anti-money laundering (AML) and know-your-customer (KYC) rules.

- **Lack of Legal Clarity**: One of the biggest challenges in DeFi is the lack of clear legal frameworks. In many countries, regulators are still trying to figure out how to treat decentralized platforms. For example, in the United States, the **Securities and Exchange Commission (SEC)** has yet to clearly define whether certain DeFi tokens are classified as securities. This uncertainty can create challenges for investors who are unsure whether they are complying with regulations when participating in DeFi activities.
- **Anti-Money Laundering (AML) and Know-Your-Customer (KYC) Rules**: Traditional financial institutions are required to comply with strict AML and KYC regulations, which help prevent money laundering and fraud. DeFi platforms, however, often don't have these same requirements, as users can interact with platforms anonymously through their wallets. This lack of oversight can make DeFi an attractive avenue for illicit activities, such as money laundering or terrorist financing, which raises concerns among regulators.
- **Regulatory Crackdowns**: Some governments are starting to take a more active role in regulating DeFi. For example, China has banned cryptocurrency trading and mining, and in the U.S., the IRS is pushing for better reporting of cryptocurrency transactions for tax purposes. As the DeFi space grows, there is likely to be increased regulatory pressure, and new laws could emerge to ensure that DeFi platforms comply with existing financial regulations.
- **Global Discrepancies**: Different countries have different approaches to regulating cryptocurrency and DeFi. While some countries, like El Salvador, have embraced Bitcoin and crypto, others, like India and China, have imposed bans

or strict restrictions. This creates a fragmented regulatory landscape where DeFi projects need to navigate complex legal systems across multiple jurisdictions. For global DeFi projects, this lack of regulatory uniformity can be difficult to manage, and changes in regulations could potentially have a significant impact on their operations.
- **Risk of Over-Regulation**: On the flip side, there's the risk that over-regulation could stifle innovation. If DeFi platforms are forced to adhere to heavy regulatory requirements, it could limit their ability to operate freely, reducing the decentralized nature of these systems. Over-regulation could also push DeFi projects to move to jurisdictions with more favorable laws, further complicating the global landscape.

While DeFi offers innovative solutions and new opportunities for financial freedom, it also comes with significant risks and challenges. Security issues, such as vulnerabilities in smart contracts, rug pulls, and flash loan attacks, can result in serious financial losses for users. Additionally, the lack of clear regulation and oversight creates uncertainty and increases the potential for illicit activities.

As the DeFi space continues to grow, it is likely that security protocols will improve, and regulatory frameworks will evolve to address these challenges. However, it's important for users to stay informed and be cautious when participating in DeFi. By understanding the risks involved, users can make smarter decisions and protect themselves from potential losses while still enjoying the benefits that DeFi has to offer.

5

Chapter 4: NFTs – Beyond the Hype

Understanding NFTs

Non-Fungible Tokens (NFTs) have taken the world by storm in recent years, especially in the realms of art, gaming, and digital ownership. While they might seem like a complex concept at first, NFTs are easier to understand when broken down into their basic components and applications. In this section, we'll dive into what NFTs are, explore the various use cases, and introduce you to the major marketplaces where NFTs are bought and sold.

What is an NFT?

An **NFT**, or Non-Fungible Token, is a unique digital asset that represents ownership of a specific item or piece of content, such as art, music, video clips, or even virtual real estate. Unlike cryptocurrencies like Bitcoin or Ethereum, which are fungible (meaning each unit is the same as every other unit), NFTs are **non-fungible**, meaning each one is distinct and cannot be replaced by another.

The uniqueness of an NFT is stored on the blockchain, a secure, decentralized ledger that records all transactions and verifies ownership. This means that, when you buy an NFT, you are not just purchasing a file; you are buying the verified ownership rights to that specific item. Although digital content like images or music can be copied and shared freely, the NFT provides proof that you are the **original owner** of that item on the blockchain.

NFTs are typically created (or "minted") on blockchain platforms that support smart contracts, with **Ethereum** being the most popular blockchain for NFTs. However, other blockchains, such as **Binance Smart Chain**, **Solana**, and **Tezos**, are also becoming popular due to their lower transaction fees and faster processing times.

One of the key features of NFTs is their **provable scarcity**—there's only one original version of a given item (although, in some cases, multiple editions may exist). This scarcity creates value, particularly in the world of collectibles, where rarity often drives demand.

Use Cases for NFTs

NFTs are much more than just digital art; they are opening up new possibilities in various industries by offering verifiable ownership and unique digital assets. Let's take a look at some of the most prominent use cases for NFTs:

1. **Digital Art and Collectibles**: NFTs are most famously associated with digital art, allowing artists to sell their works as exclusive, verifiable items. Each NFT artwork is unique and cannot be replicated, creating a new form of scarcity in the digital world. Platforms like **OpenSea** and **Rarible** allow artists to mint, showcase, and sell their digital art as NFTs. Notable sales, such as Beeple's digital collage "Everydays: The First 5000 Days," which sold for $69 million, have brought NFT art into the spotlight.
2. **Gaming**: In the gaming industry, NFTs are revolutionizing how in-game items and assets are bought, sold, and traded. Players can own items like weapons, skins, land, or characters as NFTs. These items can be bought, sold, or even used in different games, creating a cross-game economy. For example, in the game **Axie Infinity**, players can own, breed, and battle creatures (called Axies), with each Axie being an NFT. This creates a true sense of ownership for players, and some rare Axies can fetch significant prices.
3. **Virtual Real Estate**: Another growing use case for NFTs is in the ownership of virtual real estate in online worlds like **Decentraland** and **The Sandbox**. These platforms allow users to buy, sell, and build on virtual plots of land, with each plot represented as an NFT. Just like real-world real estate, the value of virtual land can fluctuate depending on location, demand, and development potential.
4. **Music and Media**: NFTs are making waves in the music industry, allowing artists to sell music, concert tickets, and exclusive content directly to their fans. For example, an artist can release an album as an NFT, providing buyers with exclusive access to the music, videos, and other bonus

content. NFTs can also be used as **royalty-generating assets**, where the original creator can earn royalties every time the NFT is resold.

5. **Identity and Certification**: NFTs can be used to prove ownership of a wide range of assets outside of the digital realm. For example, NFTs could represent a certificate of authenticity for physical goods like luxury items or even academic achievements. By tying physical assets or achievements to NFTs, owners can have verifiable proof of ownership and origin, reducing the risk of fraud.

6. **Tokenization of Real-World Assets**: NFTs also allow for the tokenization of physical assets, such as real estate, artwork, or even cars. By creating an NFT that represents ownership of a physical asset, individuals can trade these assets more easily, increasing liquidity and making it simpler for investors to gain exposure to traditionally illiquid markets.

Major NFT Marketplaces

To buy, sell, and trade NFTs, you need access to NFT marketplaces. These platforms serve as the online spaces where NFT creators can list their items, and buyers can browse and make purchases. Here are some of the most popular NFT marketplaces where you can start your NFT journey:

1. **OpenSea**: OpenSea is one of the largest and most popular NFT marketplaces. It supports a wide range of NFTs, including art, collectibles, and virtual real estate. OpenSea

is built on the Ethereum blockchain but also supports other blockchains like Polygon and Klaytn. It allows users to browse collections, create, buy, and sell NFTs, with a user-friendly interface that makes it easy to get started.
2. **Rarible**: Rarible is a decentralized marketplace that allows anyone to create, buy, and sell NFTs. It's particularly popular with artists and creators because it gives them more control over the creation process. Rarible also has its own governance token, **$RARI**, which allows users to participate in the decision-making process for the platform.
3. **SuperRare**: SuperRare is a curated NFT marketplace that focuses specifically on high-quality digital art. Each artwork on SuperRare is unique, and the platform only allows a select group of artists to mint and sell their work. SuperRare is known for its focus on creating a more art-centric environment, and its artworks often fetch higher prices than those on more general marketplaces.
4. **Foundation**: Foundation is another art-focused NFT platform that allows creators to mint and sell their digital art as NFTs. Unlike some other platforms, Foundation is an invite-only marketplace, where artists must be invited by other creators to list their work. This exclusivity has helped it build a reputation for high-quality digital art and collectible pieces.
5. **Nifty Gateway**: Nifty Gateway is a platform for buying and selling NFTs created by artists and brands. It's known for hosting **"drops"**, which are limited-time sales events where artists release a collection of NFTs. Nifty Gateway also offers **"gateway NFTs"** that can be purchased with credit cards, making it more accessible to newcomers who

may not be familiar with cryptocurrency.
6. **Axie Marketplace**: As part of the **Axie Infinity** ecosystem, the Axie Marketplace is where players can buy, sell, and trade Axies (the creatures used in the game) and other in-game assets. It's an integral part of the Axie Infinity gaming experience, allowing users to participate in the virtual economy and earn money by breeding and battling Axies.

NFTs are transforming the digital landscape by offering unique and verifiable ownership of digital assets. From digital art and collectibles to gaming items and virtual real estate, NFTs are enabling creators and users to engage in new forms of ownership and trade. As the NFT market continues to grow, it will likely open up even more opportunities for innovation and expansion in the world of digital goods.

By understanding what NFTs are, their various use cases, and the major marketplaces where they are bought and sold, you can start exploring this exciting new space and consider how NFTs might fit into your own digital collection, investment strategy, or creative endeavors.

NFT Investment Strategies

NFTs have captured the attention of investors, artists, and collectors alike due to their potential to generate significant returns. However, as with any emerging market, investing in NFTs requires careful consideration. Understanding how to assess the value of an NFT and being aware of the risks involved are essential steps to ensure that your investment strategy is well-informed and aligned with your goals. In this section, we'll explore how to assess the value of NFTs and discuss the risks associated with NFT investments.

Assessing Value

Assessing the value of an NFT is not always straightforward. Unlike traditional investments, such as stocks or bonds, NFTs are unique digital assets, and their value is often driven by factors that can be difficult to quantify. Here are some important factors to consider when evaluating the potential value of an NFT:

1. Scarcity and Rarity

Just like with physical collectibles, scarcity plays a major role in the value of an NFT. If an NFT is one of a kind or part of a limited collection, its rarity can make it more valuable. This is particularly true in the world of art and collectibles, where limited edition pieces or exclusive works tend to fetch higher prices. Always check the number of editions available for a particular NFT, as more common items may not appreciate as significantly in value.

2. Creator or Artist Reputation

The reputation of the creator or artist behind an NFT is one of the biggest determinants of its value. Well-known artists, musicians, or creators often have a loyal following that can drive demand for their NFTs. If an NFT is created by a famous artist or someone with a strong fanbase, the potential for appreciation in value is higher. For example, pieces by digital artists like Beeple or Pak have gained massive attention and sold for millions of dollars.

3. Utility and Use Case

Some NFTs have intrinsic value beyond just ownership. These NFTs may provide access to exclusive content, experiences, or membership in a community. For instance, owning certain NFTs can grant access to special events, games, or services. NFTs tied to virtual real estate or in-game assets that offer utility in the context of a game or metaverse environment can be valuable because of their practical applications in the digital world.

4. Historical Significance

NFTs tied to key moments or historical events in the digital world can also have increased value. For example, early NFTs from the inception of platforms like CryptoPunks or Decentraland hold historical significance within the blockchain and digital art community. Just as vintage physical collectibles gain value over time, NFTs that represent milestones in the evolution of blockchain technology or digital culture can see their value rise as they become more historically significant.

5. Market Demand and Trends

Like any asset, the value of NFTs is influenced by market demand. Trends in the NFT space can shift quickly, and what is popular today may lose appeal tomorrow. Keep an eye on broader trends in the NFT market and try to gauge the level of interest in a particular category or artist. Additionally, the success of a specific marketplace or platform can impact the liquidity and demand for NFTs. Understanding market sentiment and staying up to date with the latest developments can help you make better investment decisions.

6. Community and Social Proof

NFTs that are associated with strong, engaged communities tend to be more valuable. For example, NFTs linked to popular communities like Bored Ape Yacht Club or Axie Infinity have value because of the social networks and fanbases built around them. These communities help maintain the value of the NFTs by creating demand for the items and giving them cultural relevance. A strong and active community can play a major role in an NFT's long-term value.

Risks of NFTs

While NFTs offer exciting investment opportunities, they come with several risks that investors should consider before diving into this space. Here are the key risks to keep in mind when investing in NFTs:

CHAPTER 4: NFTS – BEYOND THE HYPE

1. Market Volatility

The NFT market can be highly volatile. Prices can fluctuate dramatically in a short period, and there are no guarantees that an NFT will appreciate in value over time. This volatility can be attributed to a variety of factors, such as changes in market trends, the hype surrounding specific artists or collections, and the speculative nature of many NFT investments. While some investors have seen significant returns, others have experienced sharp losses. If you're considering investing in NFTs, it's important to be prepared for the possibility of price swings and to only invest what you can afford to lose.

2. Illiquidity

Unlike stocks or bonds, which can be easily bought or sold on established exchanges, NFTs can be much harder to liquidate quickly. Although there are marketplaces like OpenSea, Rarible, and Foundation where you can buy and sell NFTs, finding a buyer who is willing to pay the price you want can be difficult, especially for niche or lesser-known NFTs. Additionally, the transaction fees on some NFT platforms can be high, particularly on Ethereum-based platforms, making it more costly to buy and sell NFTs. If you need to sell your NFTs quickly, you may be forced to accept a lower price than what you initially paid.

3. Scams and Fraud

As with any emerging market, the NFT space is susceptible to scams and fraud. "Rug pulls," where creators suddenly disappear with the funds after selling NFTs, are a real concern. Additionally, counterfeit NFTs can be sold to unsuspecting buyers, who may purchase an NFT that appears legitimate but is actually a fake or unauthorized copy. To protect yourself, it's essential to do thorough research on the creator, project, and marketplace before making a purchase. Look for verified collections and check if the NFT has been audited by a trusted source.

4. Lack of Regulation

NFTs currently exist in an unregulated market, which means there are few legal protections for investors. If an NFT project fails, gets hacked, or the creator disappears, there may be little recourse for the buyer. The regulatory landscape for NFTs is still developing, and it's unclear how governments will eventually regulate them. Without clear regulations, investors face legal uncertainty when it comes to issues like intellectual property rights, fraud, and taxation.

5. Environmental Impact

NFTs, particularly those built on the Ethereum blockchain, can have a significant environmental impact due to the energy-intensive nature of the proof-of-work consensus mechanism used by Ethereum. While Ethereum is transitioning to a more eco-friendly proof-of-stake system, the environmental impact of NFTs has been a source of concern for some investors and environmental activists. If you're concerned about the environmental footprint of your investments, it may be worth considering NFTs minted on more energy-efficient blockchains, such as **Tezos** or **Flow**.

6. Technological Risks

NFTs are still a relatively new technology, and there is a risk that the platforms or standards they rely on could change or become obsolete. For example, while Ethereum is the most widely used blockchain for NFTs, it is possible that newer technologies or blockchains could disrupt the market in the future. Additionally, the platforms where NFTs are bought and sold may face security breaches, technical failures, or other issues that could affect the value or availability of your assets.

In conclusion, while NFTs offer exciting investment opportunities, they come with inherent risks that investors must carefully consider. Assessing the value of an NFT involves understanding factors like rarity, creator reputation, utility, and market demand. However, investors should be mindful of the volatility of the NFT market, the potential for scams, and the regulatory uncertainties that exist in this space.

Before making an NFT investment, it's important to do thorough research, diversify your investments, and be prepared for potential losses. As with any investment, having a well-thought-out strategy and being aware of the risks can help you navigate the NFT market with confidence.

The Future of NFTs

The world of NFTs is still in its early stages, yet it is already changing the way we think about ownership, value, and digital assets. As technology evolves and new use cases emerge, NFTs are set to become an even more integral part of various industries. In this section, we'll explore how NFTs might evolve in the future, including the expanding use cases for NFTs and their growing impact on different industries.

Expanding Use Cases

While NFTs are most commonly associated with art, gaming, and collectibles, their potential applications go far beyond these areas. As blockchain technology continues to advance, NFTs are likely to become embedded in many other aspects of our digital and physical lives. Here are a few of the promising ways in which NFTs could expand:

1. Tokenization of Physical Assets

One of the most exciting future developments for NFTs is the ability to tokenize physical assets. This means that real-world items like real estate, luxury goods, and even cars could be represented by NFTs on the blockchain. Tokenizing these assets would make it easier to buy, sell, and trade them, providing a more efficient and transparent way to transfer ownership. For example, real estate transactions could be streamlined by using

NFTs to represent ownership of property, eliminating the need for complex paperwork and intermediaries.

2. Intellectual Property and Licensing

NFTs have the potential to revolutionize how intellectual property (IP) is managed and licensed. By creating NFTs that represent IP rights, creators and businesses could easily track ownership and ensure that royalties are distributed fairly. This could be particularly impactful in industries like music, where artists struggle to retain control over their work and receive fair compensation. NFTs could also be used to establish clearer licensing agreements, allowing creators to easily sell or lease the rights to their work while maintaining control over how it is used.

3. Metaverse Integration

The concept of the **metaverse**—a fully immersive, virtual world where people can interact, create, and own digital assets—is gaining momentum, and NFTs are poised to play a crucial role in this space. In the metaverse, NFTs could represent everything from virtual land and clothing to avatars and art. These digital assets would be fully owned by users, enabling them to customize their experiences and even trade their assets across different virtual environments. As the metaverse grows, NFTs could become the foundation for a new digital economy where people can earn, trade, and monetize their assets in immersive virtual worlds.

4. Enhanced Digital Identity

In the future, NFTs could be used to establish and protect **digital identities**. Instead of relying on traditional forms of identification like passwords or social security numbers, NFTs could represent a person's digital identity, providing a secure and verifiable way to prove identity online. This could be particularly useful for online platforms, where users could prove their identity without relying on centralized authorities, making identity management more private and secure. NFTs could also be used to grant access to exclusive communities or platforms, creating a new way of managing online access and reputation.

5. Sustainability and Carbon Offsetting

As the world becomes more aware of environmental concerns, NFTs could play a role in sustainability efforts. Some NFT platforms are already looking for ways to offset the carbon footprint of their transactions, using blockchain technologies that are more energy-efficient than the current Ethereum-based networks. In the future, NFTs could be used to track and verify carbon credits, allowing individuals and businesses to buy and sell NFTs tied to verified sustainability projects. This could help make the digital asset space more eco-friendly and align it with the growing demand for responsible investing and business practices.

Impact on Industries

NFTs are not just changing the world of art or gaming—they are impacting a wide range of industries. As NFTs continue to mature, their influence is likely to grow across various sectors, creating new opportunities and challenges for businesses and consumers alike.

1. Entertainment and Media

NFTs have already begun to make a significant impact on the entertainment and media industries, and their role is likely to expand in the coming years. In the music industry, for example, NFTs are being used to sell exclusive content, concert tickets, and even virtual meet-and-greets. This allows artists to engage directly with their fans, bypassing traditional distribution channels and retaining more control over their work. NFTs could also be used to grant access to special experiences, such as virtual concerts or behind-the-scenes content, creating new ways for fans to connect with their favorite performers.

In film and television, NFTs could provide a new way for studios and independent filmmakers to fund projects. By offering limited edition NFTs related to a film or show, creators could raise funds directly from their audience, offering them a stake in the success of the project. This could lead to new models for financing, distribution, and fan engagement in the entertainment industry.

2. Fashion and Luxury Goods

The fashion industry is increasingly exploring the potential of NFTs, particularly in the area of digital fashion. Virtual fashion items, such as clothing and accessories for avatars or virtual environments, are already being sold as NFTs. This trend is expected to grow as more people engage with the metaverse and other virtual platforms. NFTs could offer a new way for brands to engage with consumers by providing exclusive digital items that can only be accessed by owning a specific NFT.

For luxury goods, NFTs could be used to verify the authenticity of high-end products like watches, handbags, and jewelry. By attaching an NFT to a luxury item, buyers can ensure that the item is genuine and not a counterfeit. This could help reduce the prevalence of fake luxury goods and increase consumer confidence in purchasing expensive items.

3. Real Estate

The real estate industry stands to benefit significantly from the adoption of NFTs. As mentioned earlier, NFTs could be used to represent ownership of physical property, making the buying and selling of real estate faster, more transparent, and more accessible. NFTs could streamline property transactions by automating parts of the process, such as verifying ownership and transferring assets. Additionally, NFTs could make it easier for people to invest in real estate by enabling fractional ownership, where investors can purchase shares in a property through NFTs and earn a return on their investment.

4. Healthcare and Pharmaceuticals

In the healthcare industry, NFTs could provide a secure and efficient way to store and share medical records. By using NFTs to represent patient data, individuals would have more control over their medical information and could share it with healthcare providers as needed. This would improve privacy and security, as well as reduce the risk of errors or fraud. NFTs could also be used to track the provenance of pharmaceuticals, ensuring that drugs are sourced from legitimate suppliers and reducing the risk of counterfeit medications.

5. Finance and Investment

The financial industry is also exploring the potential of NFTs. In addition to being used as investment assets themselves, NFTs could represent ownership of other financial products, such as stocks, bonds, or even commodities. Fractional ownership of NFTs could allow investors to buy into high-value assets, such as art or real estate, without needing to purchase the entire asset. Additionally, the rise of decentralized finance (DeFi) platforms is likely to drive further integration of NFTs in the financial world, as NFTs can be used to represent collateral for loans or as part of yield farming strategies.

6. Supply Chain and Logistics

NFTs could help transform supply chain management by offering a transparent, immutable way to track the journey of goods from manufacturer to consumer. By linking NFTs to physical goods, companies could create a verifiable record of a product's origin, ensuring its authenticity and quality. This could be especially useful for industries like food, pharmaceuticals, and luxury goods, where traceability is critical.

The future of NFTs holds incredible promise. As use cases continue to expand and more industries embrace the technology, NFTs will likely become a foundational element of the digital economy. Whether they're being used to tokenize physical assets, create new forms of entertainment, or improve supply chain transparency, NFTs are transforming the way we think about ownership, value, and digital interactions.

As we move forward, it's important to keep an eye on the ongoing developments in the NFT space and consider how these advancements may impact various industries. Whether you're an investor, creator, or tech enthusiast, the future of NFTs offers exciting possibilities that are still unfolding.

6

Chapter 5: Next-Generation Investment Opportunities

Exploring Emerging Crypto Sectors

As the world of cryptocurrency continues to evolve, new sectors are emerging that promise to reshape the future of digital assets and investment. Among the most exciting of these are the realms of gaming, the metaverse, and the integration of artificial intelligence (AI) with blockchain technology. These sectors not only represent cutting-edge innovation but also present unique investment opportunities. In this section, we'll explore these emerging crypto sectors and what they mean for investors looking to capitalize on the next generation of digital assets.

Gaming and Metaverse Projects

The gaming industry has already embraced cryptocurrency and blockchain technology, with some of the most successful projects offering players the chance to earn, trade, and own in-game assets. However, the true potential of gaming in the world of crypto lies in the rise of the **metaverse**—a virtual world where people can interact, work, and play in fully immersive environments. Blockchain technology and NFTs (non-fungible tokens) are key to the metaverse's success, offering players a way to own, trade, and monetize their digital assets.

1. Blockchain-Based Gaming

Blockchain-based games are revolutionizing the gaming industry by allowing players to have true ownership of in-game assets. Traditionally, players spend hours, even days, to acquire rare items or characters, but they have no real control over these assets, as everything is owned by the game developers. With blockchain-based games, assets like skins, weapons, and characters can be tokenized as NFTs, meaning that players can buy, sell, and trade them freely on various marketplaces.

These games allow players to earn real-world value from their in-game activities, creating opportunities for "play-to-earn" models. Some games even offer players a chance to earn cryptocurrency by completing in-game tasks or challenges. This shift from traditional gaming models to blockchain-powered games provides new avenues for both gamers and investors, as the value of in-game items can increase based on demand and rarity.

One notable example is **Axie Infinity**, a blockchain-based game that allows players to breed, battle, and trade virtual creatures called Axies. Players can earn **Smooth Love Potion (SLP)** tokens, which can be traded for real-world currency, making it one of the most popular play-to-earn models in the crypto space.

2. Metaverse and Virtual Real Estate

The **metaverse** is an interconnected virtual world where users can own virtual property, interact with other users, and even create digital goods or services. The growth of the metaverse is a major trend in the crypto space, as platforms like **Decentraland** and **The Sandbox** allow users to buy, sell, and develop virtual land using NFTs. These virtual worlds create immersive experiences where players can engage in social, entertainment, and business activities.

Virtual real estate is becoming a hot commodity in the metaverse, with investors purchasing digital land to either hold as an asset or to develop into virtual spaces like shops, galleries, or entertainment venues. Just as physical real estate can generate rental income or increase in value over time, virtual land in the metaverse can also appreciate, creating opportunities for those who are early adopters of these virtual platforms.

For investors, the metaverse offers a new kind of market where digital assets, virtual real estate, and even virtual businesses can be traded or developed. The potential for innovation in this sector is vast, and the market is still in its infancy, making it an exciting opportunity for those looking to get in early.

3. Gaming NFTs and Cross-Platform Use

As gaming and NFTs continue to intertwine, new opportunities are emerging to bridge different gaming ecosystems. Cross-platform NFTs allow players to use their assets across various games, creating a new level of interoperability. This could lead to a future where digital assets are not restricted to one game or environment but can be used across multiple platforms, giving players more flexibility and value in their virtual items.

The rise of gaming guilds, platforms that organize and manage player communities, is also boosting the growth of crypto in gaming. These guilds often invest in NFTs and other in-game assets on behalf of players, offering them a share of the earnings from selling or trading those assets. This concept opens the door for investors who want to get involved in the gaming sector but may not want to play the games themselves.

AI and Blockchain Integration

The integration of **artificial intelligence (AI)** and **blockchain technology** is one of the most promising frontiers in the world of cryptocurrency and digital assets. AI has the ability to process vast amounts of data, learn from patterns, and make intelligent decisions, while blockchain provides a secure, transparent, and decentralized way to store and transfer data. When combined, these two technologies have the potential to unlock new use cases, improve existing systems, and create opportunities for innovation across industries.

CHAPTER 5: NEXT-GENERATION INVESTMENT OPPORTUNITIES

1. AI-Powered Blockchain Solutions

AI and blockchain are complementary technologies that can enhance one another. AI can improve blockchain in several ways, such as optimizing transaction speeds, improving security, and enhancing scalability. AI-powered algorithms can be used to predict market trends, identify vulnerabilities in blockchain networks, or automate processes such as smart contract execution. The combination of these technologies can lead to smarter, faster, and more efficient blockchain applications.

For example, AI can be used to analyze large datasets stored on blockchain networks, providing insights and helping to make better decisions. This could be useful in areas like finance, where AI could help optimize trading strategies or detect fraud in real time. In supply chain management, AI can analyze blockchain-based data to predict potential disruptions and optimize inventory management.

2. AI-Driven Decentralized Applications (dApps)

Blockchain-based applications, known as **decentralized applications (dApps)**, are already disrupting a variety of industries, from finance to gaming. The addition of AI to dApps can enhance their functionality by enabling them to adapt to changing conditions, predict outcomes, and improve user experiences. For instance, AI-powered dApps could be used in finance to automate trading, create personalized investment strategies, or optimize lending protocols.

The intersection of AI and blockchain could also lead to more advanced and automated smart contracts. Smart contracts are self-executing agreements that automatically execute actions once certain conditions are met. With AI, these contracts could become more flexible, learning from previous transactions and adapting to new scenarios in real time.

3. AI in Blockchain-Based Security

One of the key challenges in the blockchain space is ensuring the security of transactions and digital assets. AI can help address these challenges by improving the detection of suspicious activities, preventing hacks, and identifying vulnerabilities in blockchain protocols. AI algorithms can monitor blockchain networks for unusual patterns of behavior or malicious activity, enabling quicker responses to potential threats.

Additionally, AI can improve the management of private keys, wallets, and other sensitive information. Blockchain-based systems can be made more intelligent and secure with AI-powered tools, reducing the risk of fraud and theft in the crypto space.

AI and Blockchain for Data Privacy

Data privacy is becoming an increasing concern as digital interactions grow. AI and blockchain can work together to create more secure and private data-sharing systems. Blockchain's decentralized nature ensures that no central authority has control over sensitive information, while AI can be used to analyze data without compromising privacy. This could be particularly valuable in industries like healthcare, finance, and personal identity management, where data privacy is crucial.

For example, AI could be used to ensure that data stored on a blockchain is anonymized and protected while still allowing for valuable insights to be derived. AI-driven algorithms could also allow individuals to control and monetize their personal data securely, providing a new model for data ownership and privacy.

In conclusion, gaming, the metaverse, and the integration of AI with blockchain technology represent some of the most exciting and promising emerging sectors in the world of cryptocurrency. As gaming evolves into blockchain-based play-to-earn models, virtual real estate becomes more valuable in the metaverse, and AI enhances blockchain's capabilities, these sectors offer vast opportunities for investors and tech enthusiasts alike.

By understanding and exploring these emerging trends, investors can position themselves at the forefront of the next wave of crypto innovation. Whether you're looking to invest in blockchain-based games, explore virtual real estate in the metaverse, or tap into the potential of AI and blockchain integration, these emerging sectors hold significant promise for the future of digital assets.

Diversifying Your Portfolio

Diversification is one of the most important strategies in investing, especially when dealing with high-volatility assets like cryptocurrencies. In this section, we will explore the importance of portfolio allocation and some advanced strategies for building a well-diversified crypto portfolio. The goal is to reduce risk while maximizing potential returns by spreading investments across various assets and sectors within the crypto space.

Importance of Portfolio Allocation

Portfolio allocation is all about balancing your investments across different types of assets in a way that aligns with your risk tolerance, financial goals, and time horizon. The primary reason diversification matters so much is that it helps manage risk. Cryptocurrencies, despite their incredible growth potential, are still highly volatile. Prices can swing dramatically in short periods of time, and not all cryptocurrencies behave the same way. By diversifying your portfolio, you spread that risk out.

A well-allocated portfolio allows you to capture the upside potential of the most promising crypto assets while limiting exposure to those that may be riskier or prone to sharp declines. In the crypto market, where new projects are constantly emerging, having a diversified portfolio means you aren't putting all your eggs in one basket. Instead, you're balancing between well-established cryptocurrencies like Bitcoin and Ethereum, as well as emerging tokens, DeFi projects, or NFTs that may carry more risk but offer higher potential returns.

When determining your portfolio allocation, it's important to think about your risk tolerance. If you're willing to take on more risk for the possibility of higher returns, you might allocate a larger portion of your portfolio to emerging sectors or smaller altcoins. On the other hand, if you prefer a more conservative approach, you might stick with the larger, more established cryptocurrencies that have a track record of stability, like Bitcoin and Ethereum.

A simple rule of thumb is to consider a percentage of your portfolio for high-risk, high-reward assets (like altcoins and DeFi projects) and another for more stable investments (like Bitcoin or Ethereum). Rebalancing periodically is also important, as the market can shift, and the value of different cryptocurrencies can fluctuate.

Advanced Strategies

Once you understand the basics of portfolio allocation, you can start exploring more advanced strategies to take your crypto investments to the next level. Here are a few advanced approaches to consider:

1. Staking and Yield Farming

Staking and yield farming are two strategies that allow you to earn passive income from your cryptocurrency holdings.

- **Staking** involves locking up a certain amount of a cryptocurrency to help secure the network and validate transactions. In return, you earn rewards, often in the form of additional tokens. This is popular with coins that use a Proof-of-Stake (PoS) consensus mechanism, such as Ethereum 2.0, Cardano, or Polkadot.
- **Yield farming**, on the other hand, involves providing liquidity to decentralized finance (DeFi) platforms in exchange for interest or rewards. While yield farming can provide high returns, it also comes with additional risks, such as impermanent loss or smart contract vulnerabilities. The key to success in both staking and yield farming is selecting assets with a strong foundation and understanding the risks

involved.

Incorporating staking or yield farming into your portfolio can help increase your holdings over time, even if the market is flat, making it an appealing option for long-term investors.

2. Dollar-Cost Averaging (DCA)

Dollar-Cost Averaging (DCA) is a strategy that involves investing a fixed amount of money into a particular asset at regular intervals, regardless of its price. This strategy is designed to reduce the impact of short-term market volatility and eliminate the need to time the market perfectly, which can be difficult in the fast-moving world of crypto.

DCA works well for investors who believe in the long-term potential of cryptocurrency but want to avoid making large investments when prices are at their peak. By spreading your investments over time, you are more likely to buy at a range of prices, averaging out the cost of your purchases. For example, if you decide to invest $1,000 in Bitcoin, you might break it down into 12 monthly payments of about $83. This way, you avoid the risk of buying in at a single high point.

3. Hedging with Stablecoins

Stablecoins are cryptocurrencies that are pegged to a stable asset, such as the US dollar, to reduce price volatility. Examples include **Tether (USDT)** and **USD Coin (USDC)**. Hedging with stablecoins can be a useful strategy for protecting your portfolio against sudden market swings. If the crypto market is experiencing significant downturns, converting part of your portfolio into stablecoins allows you to maintain the value of your assets without being exposed to the volatility of other cryptocurrencies.

Investors often use stablecoins to temporarily park their assets during market corrections or periods of uncertainty, before re-entering riskier positions when conditions improve. Stablecoins also provide liquidity in DeFi platforms and can be used for lending and borrowing, adding flexibility to your portfolio.

4. Diversifying Across Sectors

As the cryptocurrency space evolves, it's important to consider diversification beyond just different cryptocurrencies. The crypto world is made up of several sectors, each with unique characteristics and growth potential. By investing in various sectors, such as DeFi, NFTs, gaming, and blockchain infrastructure, you can hedge against risks that may affect one sector while capitalizing on growth in another.

For example, you might allocate part of your portfolio to traditional store-of-value cryptocurrencies like Bitcoin, but also invest in tokens related to **DeFi applications**, which have their own growth potential. Similarly, investing in **gaming tokens** or **metaverse projects** could provide exposure to new and emerging trends in the crypto space. By spreading your investments across different crypto sectors, you increase the chances of being part of a high-growth project while reducing exposure to any single sector's risk.

5. Active vs. Passive Management

When it comes to managing your crypto portfolio, you can either take an active or passive approach.

- **Active management** involves regularly buying and selling assets in an attempt to outperform the market. This strategy requires deep market knowledge and the ability to react quickly to market changes. Active investors often monitor news, trends, and technical indicators to make informed decisions about which assets to hold or sell.
- **Passive management** is a more hands-off approach, where investors hold their assets for the long term without frequently buying and selling. This strategy relies on selecting strong projects with solid fundamentals and letting them grow over time. Passive investors are less concerned with short-term price fluctuations and focus on the long-term potential of their assets.

Your choice between active and passive management will depend on your time commitment, risk tolerance, and investment goals.

In summary, diversifying your portfolio is key to managing risk while maximizing your potential returns in the world of cryptocurrency. By strategically allocating your investments, using advanced strategies like staking, yield farming, and hedging with stablecoins, and diversifying across different crypto sectors, you can build a portfolio that suits your goals and helps you navigate the volatile and rapidly changing crypto market. Always remember, diversification doesn't guarantee profits or protect against losses, but it can help you achieve a more balanced and sustainable investment strategy.

Long-Term Trends to Watch

The cryptocurrency space is constantly evolving, and the changes we see today are likely to shape the future of the industry for years to come. As an investor, staying informed about the long-term trends that could impact the market is crucial to making smart decisions. In this section, we'll explore two key long-term trends to watch: institutional adoption and technological innovations. These trends are shaping the future of crypto and have the potential to significantly influence the market's growth and stability.

Institutional Adoption

One of the most significant trends in the cryptocurrency space over the past few years has been the increasing involvement of institutional investors. For a long time, cryptocurrencies were viewed primarily as speculative assets, with limited involvement from traditional financial institutions. However, that's changing rapidly.

1. Growing Interest from Major Financial Institutions

Major banks, hedge funds, and investment firms are beginning to recognize the potential of cryptocurrencies as an asset class. Companies like **Goldman Sachs**, **Fidelity**, and **JPMorgan Chase** are now offering cryptocurrency services to their clients, including trading, investment management, and custodial services.

This shift indicates that crypto is being taken seriously by the financial mainstream, and the increasing involvement of large institutions brings more credibility and stability to the market.

2. Bitcoin as Digital Gold

Bitcoin, in particular, is seen by many institutional investors as a "digital gold" – a store of value that can serve as a hedge against inflation and economic uncertainty. As central banks around the world print more money, the value of traditional currencies may decrease over time. Bitcoin, with its fixed supply and decentralized nature, offers a potential solution for institutions seeking to protect their wealth from inflation. Many institutions are now allocating a portion of their portfolios to Bitcoin, which has helped boost its legitimacy and market value.

3. Institutional Infrastructure

The growing interest in crypto from institutional players is also driving the development of infrastructure tailored to large-scale investors. Crypto exchanges are enhancing their offerings to meet institutional requirements, such as providing better security, transparency, and compliance with regulatory standards. Additionally, institutional-grade custody solutions are emerging, allowing large investors to safely store their digital assets.

As more institutions adopt crypto and build out the necessary infrastructure, the crypto market is expected to become more liquid and stable, with larger sums of money flowing in. This could lead to increased demand for digital assets and potentially higher valuations over time.

CHAPTER 5: NEXT-GENERATION INVESTMENT OPPORTUNITIES

Technological Innovations

Cryptocurrency and blockchain technology are inherently innovative, and the pace of technological advancement in this space is incredibly fast. Innovations in areas like scalability, security, and interoperability are not only improving the functionality of cryptocurrencies but also opening up new opportunities for investors.

1. Scalability Solutions

One of the biggest challenges facing the crypto industry has been scalability. As more people adopt cryptocurrencies and use blockchain-based platforms, the existing systems sometimes struggle to handle the increasing number of transactions. This leads to slow transaction times and higher fees.

However, developers are working on several innovative solutions to address these issues. For example, the introduction of **Layer 2 solutions**, such as **Bitcoin's Lightning Network** and **Ethereum's Optimistic Rollups**, is helping scale blockchain networks to handle more transactions while reducing fees. These innovations are designed to make crypto transactions faster, cheaper, and more efficient, which is key to enabling mass adoption.

Additionally, **sharding**, which involves splitting up a blockchain network into smaller, more manageable pieces, is being tested as a way to improve scalability. If successful, these solutions could help make cryptocurrencies more usable for everyday transactions and applications, driving adoption across a wide range of industries.

2. Smart Contract Improvements

Smart contracts—self-executing contracts with the terms of the agreement directly written into code—are at the heart of many decentralized applications (dApps). Over time, developers are working on improving the functionality and reliability of smart contracts. Innovations in this area will make it easier to create complex, secure, and automated contracts without intermediaries.

The rise of **Ethereum 2.0** is one of the most significant developments in the smart contract space. Ethereum's transition from Proof-of-Work (PoW) to Proof-of-Stake (PoS) aims to reduce energy consumption while increasing transaction throughput. These upgrades will make Ethereum a more attractive platform for developers, entrepreneurs, and institutions, potentially fueling the growth of decentralized finance (DeFi) and other blockchain-based applications.

3. Interoperability Between Blockchains

Another exciting technological trend is the push for **interoperability** between different blockchain networks. Right now, many blockchains operate in isolation, which can make it difficult to transfer assets or information across platforms. Innovations in cross-chain technology aim to solve this problem by allowing different blockchains to communicate with each other seamlessly.

This will be a game-changer for the crypto space, as it will create a more connected ecosystem. Projects like **Polkadot**, **Cosmos**, and **Chainlink** are leading the charge in blockchain interoperability, and their success could pave the way for a more unified and efficient crypto market. With improved interoperability, users could move assets between blockchains without the need for third-party exchanges, creating a more fluid and efficient experience for investors and users.

4. Privacy and Security Enhancements

Privacy and security are critical concerns in the cryptocurrency space, and technological advancements are constantly being made to address these issues. **Zero-knowledge proofs (ZKPs)** are one such innovation that allows for private transactions without revealing sensitive data. ZKPs can be used to verify the authenticity of a transaction while keeping the details hidden, improving privacy without compromising security.

Additionally, **hardware wallets** and **multi-signature technology** are continuing to evolve, making it easier and safer for users to store and secure their digital assets. The increase in security features, combined with innovations like ZKPs, will help make cryptocurrency transactions more private and secure, attracting a wider range of investors who are concerned about their digital asset safety.

In conclusion, both **institutional adoption** and **technological innovations** are crucial trends to watch in the coming years. As more financial institutions enter the crypto space and blockchain technology continues to improve, cryptocurrencies are likely to become a more integral part of the global financial system. Innovations in scalability, smart contracts, interoperability, and privacy will make cryptocurrencies more practical and accessible for everyday use. These long-term trends not only offer opportunities for investors but also pave the way for the broader adoption of cryptocurrency as a mainstream asset class. By staying informed about these trends, you can position yourself to take advantage of the exciting developments unfolding in the crypto world.

7

Chapter 6: How to Stay Informed and Evolve with Crypto

Keeping Up with the Crypto World

The cryptocurrency world is evolving at an incredible pace, with new developments, trends, and technologies emerging daily. To successfully navigate this fast-moving space, it's essential to stay informed and involved. In this section, we'll explore some key strategies to help you keep up with the crypto world, focusing on valuable resources and the importance of community involvement.

Essential Resources

Staying up to date with the latest news, trends, and technical developments in cryptocurrency requires access to reliable and diverse sources of information. Fortunately, there are many resources available for both beginners and seasoned investors. Here are some of the essential types of resources you should be tapping into regularly.

1. Crypto News Websites

There are several popular websites that offer up-to-the-minute news about cryptocurrency, blockchain, and the broader financial markets. Some of the most trusted sources for crypto news include:

- **CoinDesk**: Offers daily news, analysis, and trends about the crypto market.
- **CoinTelegraph**: Another popular news site, providing in-depth articles, features, and updates on cryptocurrency and blockchain developments.
- **The Block**: Known for its high-quality research and investigative reports on the crypto industry.

These platforms help you stay on top of breaking news, government regulations, market shifts, and technological breakthroughs in the crypto space.

2. Social Media and Forums

Social media platforms, such as **Twitter**, **Reddit**, and **Telegram**, have become hubs for crypto enthusiasts, traders, and developers. Follow key thought leaders, developers, and prominent crypto figures to gain insights and updates directly from the community. Some specific places to explore:

CHAPTER 6: HOW TO STAY INFORMED AND EVOLVE WITH CRYPTO

- **Reddit's Crypto Subreddits**: Subreddits like **r/CryptoCurrency** and **r/Bitcoin** are excellent for discussions, news, and sharing personal experiences.
- **Twitter**: Many influential people in the crypto world, such as **Vitalik Buterin** (Ethereum co-founder) and **CZ** (CEO of Binance), share their thoughts, research, and market outlook.
- **Telegram Groups**: Telegram has become a hub for crypto communities and project-specific groups. Joining groups related to your investment interests can provide you with insights and real-time updates.

Social media can sometimes be overwhelming due to the volume of information, so it's crucial to focus on high-quality, well-established accounts or groups with a track record of sharing valuable content.

3. Podcasts and YouTube Channels

If you prefer more in-depth analysis or commentary, podcasts and YouTube channels can provide valuable insights from industry experts. Some highly regarded crypto podcasts and YouTube channels include:

- **Unchained**: A podcast that delves into the latest trends, projects, and regulatory issues in the crypto space.
- **Crypto Frontline**: A YouTube channel providing market analysis and educational content.
- **The Pomp Podcast**: Hosted by Anthony Pompliano, this

podcast offers interviews with key figures in the crypto industry.

These platforms allow you to learn more about crypto on the go and keep you informed during your daily commute or workout.

4. Whitepapers and Technical Documents

For those with a deeper interest in the technical side of cryptocurrency, reading **whitepapers** and **technical documentation** is key to understanding the technology behind various blockchain projects. Each cryptocurrency project typically releases a whitepaper, which outlines the problem it aims to solve, its technical approach, and other important details about the project. Some important sites to explore include:

- **GitHub**: Where many blockchain projects host their code and documentation.
- **ArXiv**: A free repository of research papers, many of which cover blockchain and cryptocurrency topics.

Reading whitepapers may seem daunting at first, but they are essential if you want to understand the underlying technology and evaluate a project's legitimacy.

5. Market Tracking Tools

Keeping track of cryptocurrency prices, market cap, and trading volumes is essential for making informed investment decisions. Some of the best tools for monitoring the crypto market include:

CHAPTER 6: HOW TO STAY INFORMED AND EVOLVE WITH CRYPTO

- **CoinMarketCap**: Provides detailed data on the price, market capitalization, and trading volume of virtually every cryptocurrency.
- **CoinGecko**: Another popular site for tracking crypto prices, as well as a wide range of metrics, including liquidity and developer activity.
- **TradingView**: A charting tool widely used by traders to analyze price trends, patterns, and market signals.

These tools are essential for day-to-day trading and investing, allowing you to track the performance of your portfolio and keep an eye on market shifts.

Community Involvement

The cryptocurrency space is built around decentralized, open-source principles, and one of the best ways to stay connected with the latest developments is through active participation in the crypto community. Engaging with like-minded individuals and experts can provide you with a wealth of knowledge and insights that might not be readily available through traditional news outlets.

1. Join Crypto Communities

One of the key strengths of the crypto space is the active, passionate communities that surround each project. Whether it's through online forums, social media groups, or local meetups, participating in these communities is a great way to stay informed and gain new perspectives.

- **Discord Servers**: Many crypto projects run their own Discord servers, where developers and enthusiasts discuss the latest updates and exchange ideas.
- **Crypto Meetups**: In many cities, there are regular in-person or virtual meetups where crypto enthusiasts share knowledge and discuss the latest trends.

These communities can provide you with valuable real-time insights, opinions, and even inside information about new projects, upcoming events, or potential market shifts.

2. Contribute to Open-Source Projects

For those who are technically inclined, contributing to open-source blockchain projects is a fantastic way to stay at the forefront of innovation. Many blockchain projects rely on open-source code, and you don't need to be a developer to contribute. You could offer help with documentation, bug testing, or even marketing. By participating, you gain firsthand experience and build a network of contacts within the community.

You can find open-source projects to contribute to on platforms like **GitHub**, where developers often post issues or tasks that need attention.

3. Stay Open to Learning

As the crypto world is still in its early stages, there's always something new to learn. Stay humble and open-minded as you explore new ideas, projects, and technologies. Follow educational platforms like **Binance Academy**, **Coinbase Learn**, and **CryptoKitties** (for NFT-related education), which offer tutorials, videos, and guides to help you stay up to date with the industry.

By continually educating yourself and learning from others in the community, you position yourself to make smarter investment decisions and take advantage of new opportunities as they arise.

In conclusion, staying up-to-date with the crypto world requires a combination of reliable resources and active community involvement. Regularly reading news, following thought leaders, using market tracking tools, and joining online or in-person communities will ensure that you are always informed about the latest developments in the crypto space. Engaging with the community, whether through social media or contributing to open-source projects, can also deepen your understanding and help you build valuable connections. By staying informed and involved, you'll be well-equipped to navigate the dynamic world of cryptocurrency.

Developing Critical Skills

As the cryptocurrency world continues to grow and evolve, developing a strong set of skills is essential to making informed decisions and staying ahead of the curve. Whether you're an investor, developer, or enthusiast, honing both your financial and technical skills will give you the knowledge and confidence to navigate this fast-paced space. In this section, we'll explore the two critical areas of skills development: financial literacy and technical skills.

Financial Literacy

In order to successfully navigate the crypto world, a solid understanding of financial concepts is crucial. The digital asset space operates in many ways like traditional financial markets, but with key differences, such as high volatility and a decentralized nature. Improving your financial literacy will help you make better decisions and manage risk more effectively.

1. Understanding Market Trends

Just like in traditional finance, understanding market trends is essential in the crypto world. You'll need to learn how to interpret market data, such as price movements, trading volumes, and market capitalization, to make informed decisions. Understanding concepts like **bull markets** and **bear markets**—terms used to describe whether prices are generally rising or falling—will also help you assess market conditions.

In crypto, markets can be more volatile, and prices can fluctuate rapidly, so staying on top of news, regulations, and emerging trends is critical. This financial literacy allows you to assess when it's the right time to buy, sell, or hold your assets.

2. Risk Management

Cryptocurrencies are known for their volatility, which can offer huge potential rewards but also significant risks. Understanding risk management techniques will help you protect your investments. Concepts like **diversification**, which involves spreading your investments across different assets to reduce risk, and **position sizing**, which involves controlling how much of your portfolio is invested in each asset, are key strategies to mitigate potential losses.

You should also be aware of **market psychology**, such as how greed, fear, and FOMO (Fear of Missing Out) can affect prices and decision-making. Understanding these psychological factors will help you avoid making emotional decisions and focus on long-term goals rather than reacting to short-term price swings.

3. Investment Strategies

Just like in traditional investing, crypto investors can benefit from developing specific investment strategies. For example, **dollar-cost averaging (DCA)** is a common strategy in which you invest a fixed amount at regular intervals, regardless of the price. This helps to avoid trying to time the market and reduces the impact of short-term volatility. Understanding different types of investment strategies, from long-term holdings (also called **HODLing**) to more active trading, will help you decide what approach works best for you.

4. Taxation and Regulatory Understanding

Another key aspect of financial literacy is understanding the tax implications of cryptocurrency investments. Since crypto is still a relatively new asset class, regulations and tax rules are still evolving. It's essential to be aware of the tax rules in your country, as cryptocurrencies are often treated as property or income and subject to capital gains taxes. Understanding how to track your transactions and report them accurately will help you avoid legal issues.

Technical Skills

While financial literacy will help you manage your investments, having a solid foundation in technical skills can take your understanding of the crypto space to the next level. Whether you're interested in crypto development, trading, or simply gaining a deeper knowledge of how blockchain works, technical skills are becoming increasingly important.

1. Understanding Blockchain Technology

At the core of cryptocurrency is blockchain technology, and having a solid understanding of how it works is essential. Blockchain is the decentralized ledger that records all transactions across a network of computers. Learning the basics of how blockchain functions—such as how **blocks** are created, how **miners** validate transactions, and how the **consensus mechanism** works—will give you a deeper understanding of how cryptocurrencies like Bitcoin and Ethereum operate.

For beginners, it's helpful to start with simple concepts such as **public and private keys**, **hashing**, and **decentralization**. Once you're familiar with the fundamentals, you can dive deeper into more complex topics like **smart contracts**, **Layer 2 solutions**, and **consensus algorithms** like Proof of Work (PoW) and Proof of Stake (PoS).

2. Learning How to Use Crypto Tools and Platforms

Another important technical skill is the ability to use crypto tools and platforms effectively. For example, knowing how to navigate **cryptocurrency exchanges** (like Coinbase, Binance, or Kraken) is essential for buying, selling, and trading digital assets. Learning how to use **wallets**, whether they are software-based or hardware-based, will ensure that you can safely store and manage your crypto.

To engage in trading, you'll need to learn how to read **charts** and use **technical analysis** tools to assess market trends. Platforms like **TradingView** offer charts and indicators to help you understand price movements and identify potential buy or sell opportunities. Learning these tools and becoming proficient in using them will improve your decision-making process.

3. Programming and Smart Contracts

For those interested in the more technical side of the crypto world, learning how to code and interact with blockchain networks can open up new opportunities. **Smart contracts** are self-executing contracts with the terms of the agreement directly written into code, and they are at the heart of decentralized applications (dApps).

Languages like **Solidity** (used for Ethereum-based smart contracts) are essential for developers who want to create decentralized applications. Having programming knowledge allows you to understand how smart contracts function and how they can be applied to different use cases.

4. Understanding Crypto Security

Security is one of the most important aspects of cryptocurrency. Because crypto is decentralized, it's your responsibility to protect your assets. Gaining technical knowledge about **private keys**, **two-factor authentication (2FA)**, and **multi-signature**

wallets is essential for keeping your assets safe.

You should also be aware of potential threats, such as **phishing attacks**, **malware**, and **scams**, which are unfortunately prevalent in the crypto space. Learning about best practices for online security and how to protect your digital assets will help you avoid losing your investments to hackers or fraudsters.

In conclusion, developing both financial and technical skills is crucial for anyone looking to succeed in the world of cryptocurrency. Financial literacy will help you manage risk, develop effective investment strategies, and understand market trends, while technical skills will deepen your understanding of the technology behind crypto and provide you with the tools to use it effectively. Whether you're an investor, a developer, or just an enthusiast, continually honing these skills will enable you to make smarter, more informed decisions as you navigate the ever-evolving crypto landscape.

Future-Proofing Your Knowledge

The world of cryptocurrency and blockchain is rapidly evolving, and to remain successful and relevant, it's essential to future-proof your knowledge. This means continuously updating your skills, staying informed about new developments, and adapting to emerging technologies. In this section, we'll explore two key strategies for future-proofing your crypto knowledge: continuous education and maintaining strong security practices.

CHAPTER 6: HOW TO STAY INFORMED AND EVOLVE WITH CRYPTO

Continuous Education

As the crypto space is constantly changing, the need for continuous learning is more important than ever. New innovations, updates to existing technologies, and changes in regulations happen frequently, and staying on top of these developments is critical for making informed decisions.

1. Stay Current with Industry News

The cryptocurrency industry moves fast. Innovations that once seemed out of reach are becoming reality at a rapid pace, from **Layer 2 scaling solutions** to **Web3 technologies**. To stay ahead of the curve, make it a habit to check trusted crypto news platforms such as **CoinDesk**, **CoinTelegraph**, and **CryptoSlate** for daily updates. These platforms provide articles, market analysis, and insights into regulatory changes that affect the crypto landscape.

By regularly reading news, you'll not only learn about the latest technological breakthroughs but also about shifts in investor sentiment, industry trends, and global regulations. Being aware of these trends will help you make decisions based on up-to-date information rather than outdated assumptions.

2. Follow Thought Leaders and Experts

Alongside following news outlets, it's important to listen to and learn from experts in the field. Many prominent figures in the crypto community—such as **Vitalik Buterin** (co-founder of Ethereum) and **Andreas M. Antonopoulos** (author and speaker)—are constantly sharing their insights, thoughts, and predictions about the future of blockchain and crypto. By following them on social media or through their blogs and podcasts, you can get valuable insights directly from thought leaders who are shaping the future of this space.

Additionally, many crypto-focused companies, such as **Binance Academy** or **Coinbase Learn**, offer in-depth educational materials on everything from the basics of blockchain to advanced trading strategies and technical analysis. These platforms provide structured learning, allowing you to continuously build your knowledge in a systematic way.

3. Participate in Online Courses and Certifications

Taking part in online courses or earning certifications is another excellent way to stay on top of new developments and validate your skills. Platforms like **Coursera**, **Udemy**, and **edX** offer courses that cover a wide range of topics within the blockchain and cryptocurrency space, from beginner to expert levels. Some organizations, such as **CryptoCurrency Certification Consortium (C4)**, even offer certifications that are recognized within the industry, which can bolster your credibility as a knowledgeable participant in the crypto space.

By investing in your education and continuously upgrading your skillset, you ensure that your knowledge stays relevant and adaptable to the changing crypto landscape.

4. Engage with Emerging Technologies

To future-proof your knowledge, you also need to stay engaged with emerging technologies within the cryptocurrency world. Blockchain, for example, is just one component of the broader trend of **decentralization** that is reshaping the internet, finance, and even art (e.g., through **NFTs**). Staying on top of developments in areas like **Decentralized Finance (DeFi)**, **the Metaverse**, and **Decentralized Autonomous Organizations (DAOs)** will provide you with a better understanding of how cryptocurrency and blockchain technologies are interacting with other rapidly evolving sectors.

By continuously exploring and experimenting with new projects and ideas, you'll remain at the forefront of innovation and be able to anticipate the next big trend before it becomes mainstream.

Maintaining Security Practices

As cryptocurrencies and blockchain technologies continue to gain in popularity, so do the threats to security. Hackers, scams, and fraudsters are always looking for ways to exploit vulnerabilities in digital systems. Maintaining strong security practices is essential to safeguarding your assets and your personal information as you navigate the crypto world.

1. Secure Your Private Keys

The most fundamental aspect of securing your crypto assets is understanding how to protect your private keys. Your private key is the password to your crypto wallet, and if someone gains access to it, they can control your funds. Never share your private key, and store it in a secure location, such as a **hardware wallet** or an offline, encrypted file.

In addition, consider using **multi-signature wallets** for added security. Multi-signature wallets require multiple keys to authorize a transaction, meaning even if one key is compromised, your funds remain protected.

2. Use Two-Factor Authentication (2FA)

For added protection, always enable **two-factor authentication (2FA)** on your crypto exchanges, wallets, and other accounts related to cryptocurrency. 2FA requires you to provide two pieces of information—usually your password and a code sent to your phone or email—making it much harder for hackers to gain access to your accounts.

There are several apps available that provide 2FA codes, such as **Google Authenticator** or **Authy**, and these are generally more secure than relying on text messages for 2FA codes, which can be intercepted.

3. Be Cautious with Phishing and Scams

Phishing attacks are one of the most common ways that fraudsters trick individuals into giving away sensitive information. Be cautious when receiving unsolicited emails or messages that ask for personal details or urge you to click on links. Always verify the source of the message before clicking anything, and if the message contains links, double-check that the website is legitimate.

Additionally, be aware of common crypto scams such as **Ponzi schemes** or **rug pulls** (where project founders suddenly disappear with investors' funds). Always research projects thoroughly before investing and avoid anything that sounds too good to be true.

4. Stay Updated on Security Threats

New vulnerabilities and security threats emerge regularly, and it's crucial to stay informed about them. Follow security researchers and crypto security platforms, such as **CryptoSec**, to learn about the latest risks and best practices for protecting your assets. Also, make sure to regularly update your software and wallets, as updates often include patches for newly discovered security vulnerabilities.

Being proactive in your security measures is key to protecting your crypto holdings. Just as you stay informed about the latest trends in cryptocurrency, it's equally important to stay updated on security threats and solutions.

5. Backup Your Information

Finally, always back up your important information, including private keys, wallet passwords, and recovery phrases. Losing access to your wallet can be disastrous if you don't have a backup. Keep multiple copies in secure, offline locations to ensure you can always regain access to your funds in case of device failure or theft.

In conclusion, future-proofing your knowledge in the cryptocurrency space requires a commitment to continuous education and robust security practices. By staying informed about industry news, engaging with emerging technologies, and constantly updating your skills, you can ensure that you remain adaptable in this fast-evolving field. At the same time, maintaining strong security practices is crucial to protecting your assets and ensuring your longevity in the crypto space. By combining both of these strategies, you'll be well-positioned to thrive as the world of cryptocurrency continues to expand and evolve.

8

Conclusion: Embracing the Future of Crypto

As we conclude this journey through the world of cryptocurrency, blockchain, and decentralized technologies, it's important to take a moment to reflect on the key insights we've covered. This book has aimed to provide you with a clear and practical understanding of the crypto space, empowering you to make informed decisions and to see the big picture as this transformative technology evolves. In this final chapter, we'll summarize the key takeaways, discuss your role in the crypto ecosystem, look ahead to 2030, and share some final thoughts to guide your ongoing journey.

Key Takeaways

From the basics of blockchain to the cutting-edge concepts of DeFi, NFTs, and the future of decentralized technologies, this book has highlighted the most important aspects of the cryptocurrency space. Here are some key points to remember as you move forward:

- Blockchain is the backbone of cryptocurrency and decentralized technologies, offering a secure, transparent, and tamper-proof way to record transactions.
- Cryptocurrencies, such as Bitcoin and Ethereum, are digital assets that operate on these decentralized networks. They are changing the way we think about money, ownership, and value.
- DeFi (Decentralized Finance) offers a new way of providing financial services without intermediaries, democratizing access to financial products and creating opportunities for innovation in banking and lending.
- NFTs (Non-Fungible Tokens) have opened up new avenues for digital ownership, allowing creators and investors to tokenize unique digital assets.
- Security and education are fundamental to success in the crypto world. Protecting your assets and continuously updating your knowledge are the cornerstones of responsible participation.

As you venture further into this space, these key concepts will serve as the foundation for a deeper understanding of the crypto ecosystem and its many opportunities.

Your Role in the Crypto Ecosystem

The cryptocurrency world is vast and multifaceted, and there's a place for everyone to participate. Whether you're an investor, a developer, a creator, or just someone passionate about blockchain technology, your role in the ecosystem is important.

As an investor, you are contributing to the growth and adoption of blockchain projects by supporting innovative solutions and helping to build the future of decentralized finance. Your decisions can help shape the market and provide valuable feedback to the teams developing these technologies.

As a developer, you have the opportunity to directly impact the direction of blockchain technology by building the next generation of decentralized applications (dApps), improving security protocols, or creating new blockchain solutions that address real-world problems.

If you're a creator, NFTs provide a platform to tokenize your work, enabling direct engagement with your audience and allowing you to retain ownership of your digital assets in a way that was not possible before. The creative possibilities within the blockchain space are vast, from art to music, gaming, and beyond.

Finally, even if you're simply an enthusiast, your role in the ecosystem is still crucial. Spreading knowledge, educating others, and participating in community discussions helps to foster the growth of the crypto space. The more people who understand how blockchain works, the faster adoption will occur, and the more powerful the technology will become.

Looking Toward 2030

As we look ahead to 2030, the future of cryptocurrency and blockchain technology is incredibly exciting. We are on the cusp of a new era in digital finance, and the possibilities are endless. While we can't predict all the developments that will unfold in the next decade, several trends are already emerging that suggest where the space is heading.

1. Mainstream Adoption: By 2030, cryptocurrencies and blockchain technology are likely to be a more integrated part of our daily lives. With increasing institutional adoption and the expansion of DeFi, we may see a future where blockchain-based payments and financial services are the norm rather than the exception.
2. Regulation and Standardization: The regulatory landscape is still evolving, and by 2030, clearer global frameworks may be in place to ensure the safe and fair use of cryptocurrencies. This could help reduce risks associated with fraud and security issues, encouraging even more widespread adoption.
3. Advanced Use Cases: Blockchain will likely continue to extend beyond finance and into other industries such as healthcare, supply chain management, education, and government. New use cases, like decentralized identity management and tokenization of real-world assets, could become mainstream by 2030.
4. The Metaverse and NFTs: As the Metaverse grows and becomes a more significant part of digital life, NFTs may evolve into important assets in virtual worlds. This could open up exciting new possibilities for entertainment, social interactions, and business in virtual environments.

While we don't know exactly what the crypto world will look like in 2030, it's clear that the pace of innovation will continue, and those who are educated and engaged will be in a strong position to benefit from the opportunities that emerge.

Final Thoughts

Cryptocurrency and blockchain technology are reshaping the way we think about finance, value, and ownership. The space is filled with incredible potential, but it also comes with risks and challenges. As with any new technology, there is much to learn, and the landscape can change quickly.

By focusing on continuous education, maintaining strong security practices, and staying adaptable to the evolving ecosystem, you'll be well-positioned to succeed in the world of crypto. The key to thriving in this space is not only understanding the technology itself but also understanding how to use it responsibly and ethically.

Remember, the journey doesn't end here. The crypto world is still in its early stages, and every day brings new opportunities for innovation and growth. By staying curious, open-minded, and proactive, you'll be able to navigate the exciting changes ahead and make a lasting impact on the future of this revolutionary technology.

Thank you for taking the time to explore the world of cryptocurrency with me. The future is bright, and now it's your turn to **contribute to the next chapter in the crypto revolution.**

References

1. Nakamoto, S. (2008). Bitcoin: A Peer-to-Peer Electronic Cash System. Retrieved from https://bitcoin.org/bitcoin.p

df
2. Antonopoulos, A. M. (2017). Mastering Bitcoin: Unlocking Digital Cryptocurrencies. O'Reilly Media.
3. Tapscott, D., & Tapscott, A. (2016). Blockchain Revolution: How the Technology Behind Bitcoin and Other Cryptocurrencies is Changing the World. Penguin.
4. CoinDesk. (2024). Crypto and Blockchain News. Retrieved from https://www.coindesk.com
5. CoinTelegraph. (2024). Latest News in Blockchain and Cryptocurrency. Retrieved from https://cointelegraph.com
6. DeFilippi, P., & Wright, A. (2018). Blockchain and the Law: The Rule of Code. Harvard University Press.
7. Ethereum Foundation. (2013). Ethereum Whitepaper. Retrieved from https://ethereum.org/whitepaper
8. Binance Academy. (2024). What Are NFTs and How Do They Work? Retrieved from https://academy.binance.com
9. Wright, A., & DeFilippi, P. (2018). Blockchain and the Law: The Rule of Code. Harvard University Press.
10. Web3 Foundation. (2024). What Is Web3 and Why It Matters. Retrieved from https://web3.foundation

www.ingramcontent.com/pod-product-compliance
Lightning Source LLC
Chambersburg PA
CBHW070244220526
45465CB00004B/1522